a *Yachting Monthly* pilot

G000268906

EAST COAST RIVERS
From Southwold to the Swale

Jack H Coote (Revised by Janet Harber)

First edition, 1956;
Second edition, 1957;
Third edition, 1961;
Fourth edition (revised), 1965;
Fifth edition (revised), 1967;
Sixth edition (revised), 1970;
Reprinted, 1971;
Seventh edition (revised), 1974;
Reprinted, 1974;
Eighth edition (IALA revision), 1977;
Ninth edition, 1979;
Tenth edition (revised), 1981;
Eleventh edition (new charts), 1983;
Twelfth edition (revised), 1985;
Thirteenth edition (Navaid Review), 1988;
Thirteenth edition (revised), 1989;
Fourteenth edition, 1993
Fifteenth edition (revised by Janet Harber) 1996
Sixteenth edition 1998

Design by SMF Graphics (0181-399 6265)
Photographs by Janet Harber, except where otherwise credited

IPC Magazines Ltd, King's Reach Tower,
Stamford Street, London SE1 9LS
1998

ISBN 1-85277-078-3

Printed in Hong Kong

Cover: The moorings at Ramsholt on the River Deben in Suffolk
Back cover: Cliff Foot buoy at the entrance to Harwich Harbour – Felixtowe container terminal on the skyline

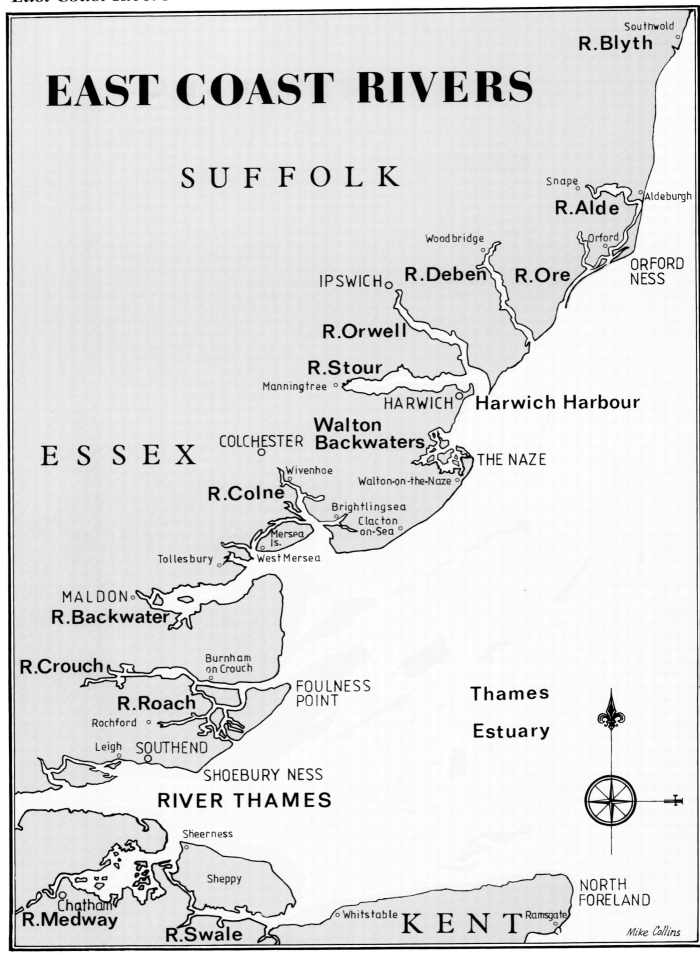

EAST COAST RIVERS

SUFFOLK

R.Blyth

Southwold

Snape

R.Alde

Aldeburgh

Woodbridge

Orford

IPSWICH

R.Deben

R.Ore

ORFORD NESS

R.Orwell

R.Stour

Manningtree

HARWICH

Harwich Harbour

Walton Backwaters

COLCHESTER

THE NAZE

ESSEX

Wivenhoe

Walton-on-the-Naze

R.Colne

Brightlingsea

Clacton on-Sea

Mersea Is.

Tollesbury

West Mersea

MALDON

R.Backwater

R.Crouch

Burnham on Crouch

FOULNESS POINT

Thames

R.Roach

Rochford

Estuary

Leigh

SOUTHEND

SHOEBURY NESS

RIVER THAMES

Sheerness

Sheppy

NORTH FORELAND

Chatham

R.Medway

Whitstable

KENT

Ramsgate

R.Swale

Mike Collins

2

East Coast Rivers

The following short extract from the earliest sailing directions for the coasts of England, written in the time of Edward IV, shows that the inshore passage along the Essex coast remains much the same after five hundred years: *'From Orfordness to Orwell wanes (shallows) the course is south-west, and it (the tide) floweth south-south-east, and in Orwell Haven within the weirs south and north; and if ye go out of Orwell wanes to the Naze ye must go south-west. From the Naze to the marks of the Spits (Spitway) your course is west-south-west, and it (the tide) floweth south and by east. Bring your marks together that the parish steeple be out (clear) by east the abbey of St Osyth, then go your course on the Spits south till you come to 10 fathoms or 12, then go your course with the Horseshoe (Shoe Spit).'*

The East Coast Rivers

The rivers and creeks, channels, guts and swatchways of the Kent, Essex and Suffolk coasts have an ancient charm and character quite unlike anywhere else. The labyrinth of offshore banks, so menacing to the eyes of deep water sailors, are a shelter to those who know them and the wandering creeks offer an endless choice of anchorage.

The revised edition of *East Coast Rivers* with its corrected charts and many new photographs, also includes a four-language glossary of pilotage terms and a tidal atlas and constants. An annual correction service to help keep this pilot book up-to-date is offered, between editions.

New Editors: Jack Coote, who died in 1993, started cruising the East Coast with his wife and two daughters, Janet and Judy, in the 1950s. He produced the first edition of *East Coast Rivers* for *Yachting Monthly* in 1956. Jack had always hoped that the constant task of revising the pilot book would eventually be taken over by his family, who had all along played an active part in the information gathering.

In 1995 with the agreement of *YM*, the 15th edition was edited and corrected by Janet Harber assisted by Judy Jones. Both daughters have carried on the family tradition of East Coast cruising in various boats of their own, always with heavily annotated copies of *East Coast Rivers* beside them in the cockpit. They plan to continue revising future editions with the help of an invaluable network of fellow East Coast sailors.

Amendment service

Like charts, pilot books need revision at intervals. During the life of an edition therefore the editors will provide correction data on request. Issued annually on or after the 1st of May in the year following the publication of this current edition, data sheet(s) may be obtained by writing to:
Judy Jones, 7 Grasmere Avenue, Felixstowe, Suffolk IP11 9SG
enclosing a cheque or PO for £1.00 and a large self-addressed and stamped return envelope.

Contents

Introduction to the 16th edition

Development over the two years since the previous edition includes a new marina in Gallions Reach on the Thames between Barking Creek and Woolwich. The extensions to the Trinity Container Terminal at Felixstowe have been completed and movements in and out of Harwich Harbour are now busier than ever. Revisions and improvements to both the text and several of the charts have been made in this latest edition. Over half the photographs have been replaced with new ones taken over the past two seasons. These include several aerial views, shot with the help of my brother-in-law, Graham Jones, who skilfully piloted us over the relevant areas on two memorable flights. The pictures of the Alde and Deben entrances were taken at the time of an astronomically low spring tide in late 1997 and show how the shoals and shingle banks have changed dramatically in recent years. I am afraid that as there was a brisk onshore breeze at the time, both Woodbridge and Orford Havens look somewhat uninviting, but I hope this will not deter yachtsmen from visiting these two rivers.

The 'Facility' boxes have been revised as Port Guides and, at the suggestion of D. W. Mangan, a reader from Rendham in Suffolk, harbourmasters' telephone numbers are now included. He is not alone in mentioning that it is often difficult to raise a marina on VHF, and that using a mobile 'phone can sometimes be more successful. It is also useful to be able to contact marinas or yacht clubs before setting out (when planning a cruise, for example) so the relevant numbers are now available with the Port Guide information.

Since Trinity House implemented their Navaid Review in 1988 and relinquished responsibility for buoying and marking a number of areas they had previously administered, responsibility for buoying such rivers as the Crouch has been transferred to the local River Authority. When yachts and local fishermen are the only users of a river, as for example on the Deben or the Alde, either the local authority, such as the Maldon District Council in the case of the Blackwater; Fairways Committees, as on the Deben, or local clubs such as the Aldeburgh Yacht Club and the Walton and Frinton Yacht Club, accept responsibility for marking the channels in their area. In the mid-'90s the Walton and Frinton Yacht Club provided a light for High Hill, the first time a buoy in the entrance to Walton Backwaters had been lit. Yachtsmen should never forget how dependent they are on such committees, clubs and local authorities.

Acknowledgements

For the 16th edition I am very grateful to Eric Stone (*Maris*) for his invaluable and regular contributions containing detailed corrections, additional information, and helpful suggestions, particularly on updating the Estuary crossings. 'Our man on the Medway', Malcolm Ritman (*Dimple*), kindly supplied some new photographs from the Kent side; Mike and Sue Ramsay (*Scilla*) once more kept us informed on the Mersea scene and went surveying up Woodrolfe Creek at low water; Michael Withers ferried us on a photo-shoot out of Shotley and patiently manoeuvred *Sula* to get the right angles. Graham Jones not only piloted me over East Coast rivers from the air, but also, with my sister Judy, piloted their boat up many a creek in the quest for the latest local knowledge. I am indebted to them, and countless other people for their help in producing up-to-date editions of *East Coast Rivers*.

If you have any local information, corrections, or amendments, please continue to send them to Judy Jones at the address given on the previous page.

Janet Harber, January 1998

Notes
Buoyage
Lateral Marks

Lateral marks are used for well defined channels and they indicate the port and starboard hands of the route to be followed.

A port hand mark is coloured red and its basic shape is can for either buoy or topmark or both.

A starboard hand mark is normally coloured green and its basic shape is conical for either buoy or topmark (point-up) or both. (Sometimes it will be permissible to use black instead of green to enhance visibility.) By night a port hand buoy is identifiable by its red light and a starboard hand by its green light.

(The West Swin, for example, is marked by a series of red can (port hand) and green conical (starboard hand) buoys.)

Cardinal Marks

Cardinal Marks are used in conjunction with the compass to indicate where there is best water. A cardinal mark is placed in one of the quadrants – N, E, S and W – and takes its name from the quadrant in which it is placed. It is safe to pass north of a N cardinal mark, east of an E cardinal mark, south of a S cardinal mark and west of a W cardinal mark.

The shape of a cardinal mark is not significant although in the case of a buoy it will be a pillar or a spar; but its black double-cone topmark is the most important feature.

The cone topmarks should be remembered:
North Points up
South Points down
East Points outwards
West Points inwards (wineglass)

Cardinal marks are used to indicate the safe side on which to pass a danger or to draw attention to a feature in a channel such as a bend or junction or the end of a shoal.

(The Whiting Bank off Orford Ness is marked by E and S Cardinal buoys)

Cardinal marks are coloured black and yellow and when lit, display a series of quick or very quick white flashes.

Other Types of Mark

There are three other categories of marks that can be used. They are: Isolated Danger Marks, Safe Water Marks and Special Marks.

A black double sphere topmark is the most important feature of an isolated danger mark which will have red and black horizontal stripes and can be erected on or moored on or above an isolated danger of limited extent such as a shoal or a rock well offshore. (The Whitaker beacon is an example.)

A Safe Water mark will be painted with red and white vertical stripes and have a single red spherical topmark. It can be used to indicate mid-channel or as a landfall buoy. (The Medway No. 1 buoy is an example.)

Finally, there is sometimes the need for special marks to indicate traffic separation, spoilground, a lightship watch buoy as well as cable or pipeline marks including outfalls. A Special mark will be yellow and will usually have a single yellow cross (X) as a topmark. (Sea Reach No. 1 buoy (Spher. Y) marking the entrance to the Yantlet dredged channel is a Special mark.) Whenever a light is shown from a Special buoy it is yellow.

Chart datum
Lowest Astronomical Tide (LAT)

Although it has the effect of indicating that some creeks, swatchways and anchorages sometimes dry out, when many of us have never seen them without water, adoption of the lowest astronomically predicted tides (LAT) as the datum for this book has been deemed necessary in order to be in accord with Admiralty charts.

Abbreviations

The abbreviations employed for indication of the shape, colour and light characteristics of buoys and marks are as follows:

Can	can shaped
Con	conical shaped
Sph	spherical shaped
R	red
G	green
Y	yellow
B	black
R W	red and white
B Y	black and yellow
B R	black and red
V S	vertical stripes
H S	horizontal stripes
Lt (or L)	light-white unless otherwise qualified eg, LtR-red light
F R	fixed red light
F G	fixed green light
Fl R	flashing red light
Fl G	flashing green light
Fl Y	flashing yellow light
Oc R	red light occulting
Oc G	green light occulting
Fl (number)	light showing given number of flashes as a group
Q	light showing group of quick flashes (50-60 per min)
V Q	light showing group of very quick flashes (100-120 per min)
L Fl	light showing long flash of not less than 2 sec
s	replaces abbreviation 'sec'
Iso	light showing equal light and dark phases

Charts

All the charts have been specially drawn in the belief that a good deal of useful information and anticipatory pleasure can be obtained from the study of them before the commencement of a passage or a cruise.

Wherever Admiralty charts are available to cover the area required, it is strongly recommended that up-dated copies of these should be used together with the charts in this book.

Bearings

The bearings given throughout the book are magnetic and the variation in the area of the Thames Estuary is approximately 4 degrees W, decreasing by about 10 minutes annually.

Tides

Although there are times when tides, as Para Handy said, 'is chust a mystery', they do tend to follow patterns that are useful to know.

Spring tides occur a day or so after both new and full moon – hence the term High Water Full and Change (H W F C).

Neap tides occur midway between each spring tide.

Remember there is always more water at low water neaps than at low water springs.

The time of High Water at any given place is approximately 50 minutes later each day.

All tidal information is approximate, so allow a safety margin whenever possible. Watch the barometric pressure – a change of one inch in pressure can make a difference of a foot in the level of water.

The level of water does not rise and fall at a constant rate during the flood or ebb tide. The amount by which a tide will rise or fall in a given time from Low or High Water can be estimated approximately by the 'Twelfths' rule, which can be simply indicated as follows:

Rise or fall during	1st hour	$\frac{1}{12}$ of range
" " " "	2nd hour	$\frac{2}{12}$ " "
" " " "	3rd hour	$\frac{3}{12}$ " "
" " " "	4th hour	$\frac{3}{12}$ " "
" " " "	5th hour	$\frac{2}{12}$ " "
" " " "	6th hour	$\frac{1}{12}$ " "

Cross Estuary Routes

We have added a route to the existing suggested courses by which the Thames Estuary might be crossed between Essex and Kent. When the cross estuary routes were first included, Jack Coote was keenly aware of the danger of seeming to encourage insufficiently experienced yachtsmen to set off across the shoals of the Thames delta without fully understanding the risks involved. In recent years, yachtsmen have had to become increasingly self-dependent in matters of navigation, as organisations like Trinity House and the Port of London Authority (which surveys most of the Thames Estuary) have been forced to reduce the scale of their activities by eliminating any marks and surveys that are not commercially necessary.

All of this means that even when equipped with the latest charts, a yachtsman must recognise that the soundings shown in a particular swatchway may well have changed since the time of the last survey. Therefore fair weather, a reliable echo-sounder, and a rising tide are more than ever essential for a safe crossing of the Estuary; if satnav or GPS are available, so much the better.

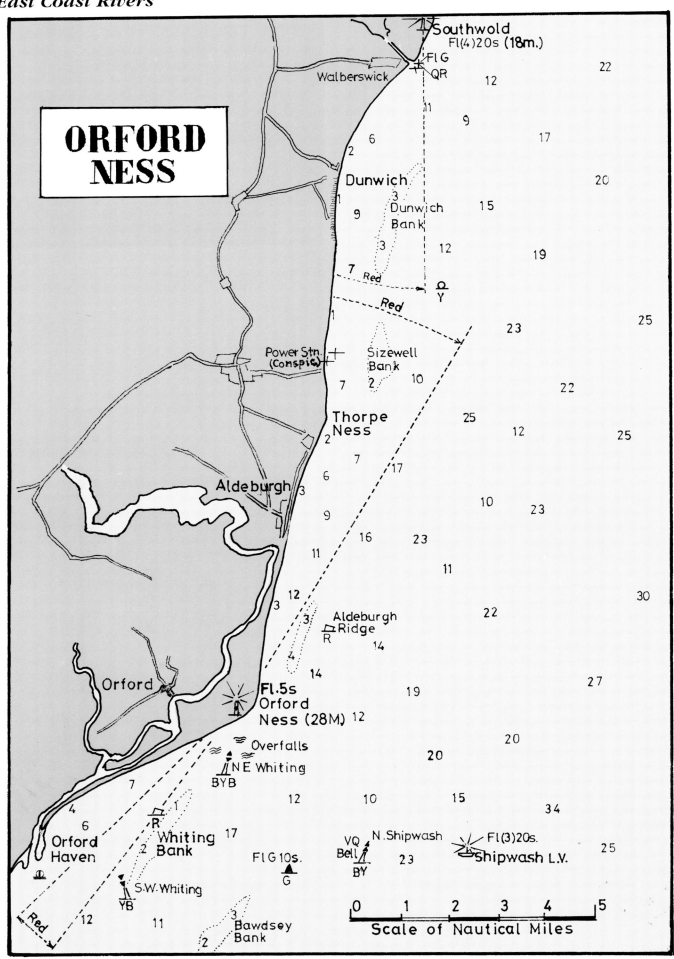

ORFORD NESS

Southwold
Fl(4)20s (18m.)
Fl G
QR

Walberswick

22

12

9

6   17

2

Dunwich   20

3   15

9   Dunwich
Bank

3   12   19

7   Red   23   25

Ω
Y

Red

1

23   25

Power Stn.
(Conspic)   Sizewell
Bank   22

7   2   10

Thorpe   25
Ness   12   25

2

7   17

6   10   23

Aldeburgh   9

3   16   23

9   11

11   22   30

12

3   Aldeburgh
3   Ridge   10
R   14

4   19   27

14

Orford   Fl.5s
Orford   20
Ness (28M) 12

Overfalls   20

NE Whiting
BYB   12   10   15   34

7   N.Shipwash   Fl(3)20s.
VQ   25
4   1   Bell   Shipwash L.V.
R   BY
6   17
Orford   23
Haven   2   Whiting
Bank   Fl G 10s.
G

S.W.Whiting
YB

Red   12   11   3   Bawdsey
Bank

2

0   1   2   3   4   5
Scale of Nautical Miles

1. Southwold

Tides: HW Dover -1.05 Range: Springs 1.9m Neaps 1.2m
Charts: Admiralty 1543, Stanford No.3, Imray C28
Waypoints: Orfordness Lighthouse 52.05.00N 01.34.60E. Southwold N Pier 52.18.77N 01.40.63E
Hazards: Entrance. Not to be attempted in strong onshore winds

owland Parker, in his book Men of Dunwich, tells how – 'On the Night after New Year's Day' in 1286, 'through the Vehemence of the Winds and Violence of the Sea' the river Blyth found its way directly out to sea between Walberswick and Southwold rather than through the port of Dunwich. The men of Dunwich did in fact manage to stop up the gap for a few years after, but on the afternoon of 14th January 1328, a NE'ly gale again coincided with the high tides of the month and the town of Dunwich was devastated; this time beyond any hope of recovery. From that time Southwold has been a port; at first for trading and fishing but in recent years simply as a pleasant haven for cruising yachts from both sides of the North Sea.

Southwold harbour is about as far north of Orfordness as Landguard Point is south of it – roughly 15 miles. There are several shoals lying a mile or so offshore between Orford Haven and Southwold. The largest of them, the Whiting Bank, is guarded at its northern end by an E Cardinal buoy and at its southern end by a S Cardinal buoy, while the red can, Whiting Hook buoy, marks the western edge of the shoal. All three buoys are unlit.

A solitary unlit red can buoy marks the eastern side of the Aldeburgh Ridge which lies about a mile offshore but has six to eight metres on its western side, very close to the shingle shore of the Ness itself. The only snag when taking this inshore course round Orfordness is that overfalls occur on the ebb.

There is one other shallow patch, the Sizewell Bank, about a mile offshore opposite the atomic power station, but this unmarked patch has some three metres over it at LWS.

It should be noted that the direction of buoyage changes to the N of Orfordness.

There is a lighthouse – Fl (4) WR – situated in the town of Southwold about a mile to the north of the harbour.

Since entry to Southwold harbour should be made on the flood (the ebb runs out at anything up to 6 knots), it will often pay when coming from the south, to use the north-going ebb and then wait off the harbour entrance for a while, either by heaving-to or lying to an anchor about a quarter of a mile S of the pierheads if the wind is light and offshore.

The best time to go in is during the second half of the flood, but whenever there is a strong wind from any direction between NE and SE, the entrance can be dangerous and certainly must not be attempted if three vertical flashing red lights are shown by night.

A flashing green light is shown from the N pier and a flashing red from the S pier.

The harbour master, Ken Howells, offers to provide up-to-date information by telephone – 01502 724712 – or on VHF Ch12. He is also willing to come out in his launch to guide yachts in if necessary.

Entrance can be made from half a mile offshore in transit with the end of the south pier. Once inside the pierheads, steer for a pile structure at the inshore end of the north pier. This staging is known as the 'Knuckle' and is marked by a beacon bearing two vertical green lights. When abreast the Knuckle, keeping just 2 metres off, change course immediately to the Lifeboat house on the north shore, then keep along the dock wall. At the end of the wall, move to the centre of the channel again and continue midway between the stagings on

At Southwold yachts lie to wooden staging by the Harbour Inn on the north bank of the river. The bailey bridge can be seen in the background

both sides. There are permanent moorings on these wooden stagings and a pontoon is reserved for visiting yachtsmen about a quarter of a mile beyond the ferry, on the north bank, just by the Harbour Inn.

Waveney District Council administer the harbour, and the harbourmaster's office is in the old Lifeboat shed near the visitors' pontoons.

Walberswick

Although most yachtsmen land on the N side of the harbour and visit Southwold, Walberswick too is a charming little place, that has attracted artists ever since the days of Charles

The yacht entering Southwold Harbour is about to pass between the pierheads

Port Guide: Southwold	
Harbourmaster	Ken Howells Tel (01502) 724712
Water	Near visitors' berth
Stores	Basic requirements from chandler, otherwise from Southwold (1 mile) EC Wed
Repairs	Repair service, slip (up to 20 ton) and 10 ton lifting hoist at Harbour Marine Services. Tel (01502) 724721
Fuel	Diesel delivered to visitors' pontoon
Transport	Railway station at Halesworth, reached by taxi or bus from Southwold, or Darsham, by taxi from Walberswick. Bus to Lowestoft
Telephones	At chandlers, near N pier and at pub
Club	Southwold Sailing Club
VHF	Ch 12, for the Harbour Master or Pilot, also Ch 9

Keene and Wilson Steer at the end of the last century. It can be reached by crossing the Bailey bridge upstream of the Harbour Inn, and walking back down the south bank of the River Blyth. Alternatively you can cross to the Walberswick side by getting the ferryman to row you over from near the fishermen's sheds.

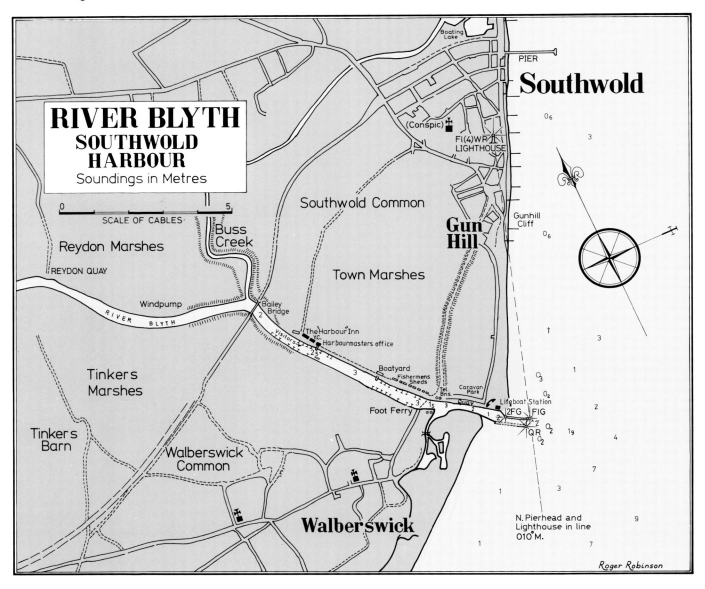

RIVER BLYTH
SOUTHWOLD
HARBOUR
Soundings in Metres

SCALE OF CABLES

Reydon Marshes

REYDON QUAY

Buss Creek

Southwold Common

Southwold

PIER

(Conspic)

Fl(4)WR
LIGHTHOUSE

Gunhill Cliff

Gun Hill

Town Marshes

Windpump

Bailey Bridge

RIVER BLYTH

Visitors

The Harbour Inn
Y.C.
Harbourmasters office

Tinkers Marshes

Boatyard
Fishermens Sheds
Tel Bns.

Caravan Park

Lifeboat Station

Foot Ferry

Quay
2FG FlG
QR

Tinkers Barn

Walberswick Common

Walberswick

N. Pierhead and Lighthouse in line 010°M.

Roger Robinson

2. Orford River

Tides (at entrance): HW Dover + 0.15 Range: Springs 2.0m Neaps 1.7m
Charts: Admiralty 2693, Stanford No. 6, Imray C28
Waypoint: Orford Haven Buoy (liable to be moved) 52.01.63N 1.27.67E
For latest position contact Thames Coastguard Frinton-on-Sea (01255) 675518
Hazards: Shoals and strong tides in entrance (Seek up-to-date information from Aldeburgh YC).
Shoal just inside entrance

Orford Haven

Orford Haven lies at the southern end of Hollesley Bay, some four or five miles N of the entrance to the Deben, but it is not easy to locate the actual entrance.

The only helpful landmarks are a Martello Tower about a mile SW of the entrance proper and a few houses in two small rows just N of the tower.

The offing buoy ('Orford Haven' Sph RWVS) is in about 6m of water at LWS and situated approximately half a mile SE of the cottages at Shingle Street.

Although given the dual names, the Ore and the Alde are merely different parts of a single river; the Ore being that part between the entrance (Orford Haven) and Randalls Point (between Orford and Slaughden Quay) while the Alde is the river thereon up to its navigable limit at Snape Bridge, a distance of about 16 miles.

As with the River Deben, the Ore reaches the sea through a narrow shingle banked outlet, and as a result there is a shingle bar and several drying and shifting shingle banks or 'knolls' in the entrance. The bar and the knolls, and the fact that the tides run in and out of the river very strongly indeed, combine to make Orford Haven rather more difficult to enter than the Deben, because there is no pilot on hand and only one leading mark compared with the two metes at Felixstowe Ferry.

The beacon (orange and white post with orange diamond shaped topmark) was erected by Trinity House in 1975 and has not been moved since.

It must never be assumed that it is safe to follow a direct course between the offing buoy and the beacon.

As the directions change each year, yachtsmen are fortunate that a survey of the entrance is carried out at the beginning of each season. The findings are incorporated in the annual Information and Guidelines leaflet, which is published by the Alde and Ore Association. This is available from the Aldeburgh Yacht Club, local chandlers, or from the association at Woodlands, Priory Road, Snape IP17 1SD – send £1.50 plus large SAE.

Orford Haven looking north at the River Ore entrance, with the Martello Tower, and coastguard cottages along the beach at Shingle Street

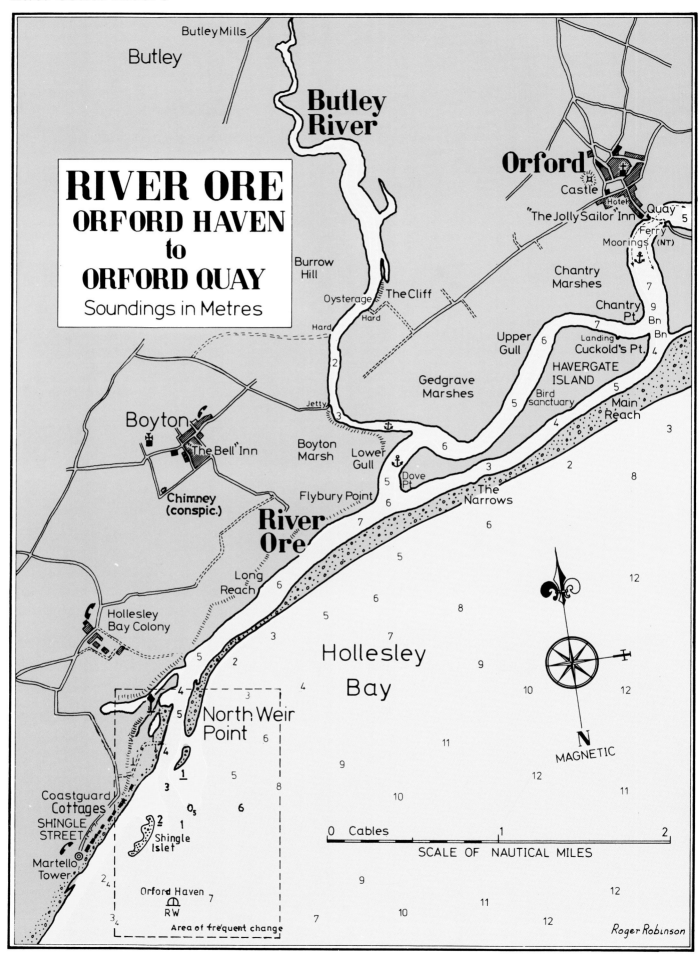

Butley Mills

Butley

Butley River

Orford

Castle

"The Jolly Sailor Inn"   Hotel   Quay   5

Moorings (NT)   Ferry

7

Chantry Marshes

Chantry Pt.   9   Bn

Bn

RIVER ORE
ORFORD HAVEN
to
ORFORD QUAY
Soundings in Metres

Burrow Hill

Oysterage   The Cliff

Hard   Hard

Upper Gull   6   Landing   7   Cuckold's Pt.   4

HAVERGATE ISLAND

Gedgrave Marshes   Bird sanctuary   5   Main Reach

2   5   5   3

Jetty   3   4   8

Boyton   6

"The Bell" Inn

Boyton Marsh   Lower Gull   6   2

Chimney (conspic.)   5   Dove Pt.   3

River Ore   Flybury Point   6   The Narrows   6

7   5

Long Reach   6   5

3   6   8

Hollesley Bay Colony   5   7

3   9

5   2   4   **Hollesley Bay**   11

North Weir Point   9

4   6   10   12

4

1   5   8   12

3   11

Coastguard Cottages   O 5   6   10

SHINGLE STREET   2   1   9

Shingle Islet   12

Martello Tower   2   4   7   11

Orford Haven   12

3   4   RW

Area of frequent change   7   10   12

12

8   3

10   12

Bn

N MAGNETIC

0   Cables   1   2

SCALE OF NAUTICAL MILES

Roger Robinson

10

Orford Haven and the entrance to the River Ore, looking south-west. This picture shows that the shoals extending from North Weir Point have moved considerably further southward in recent years

The River Ore

Within the entrance the tidal streams run very strongly indeed; probably up to 4 knots on the flood and as much as 5 knots during the latter half of a spring ebb. Because of this, entry against the ebb is virtually impossible, while departure on the ebb is certainly inadvisable.

Probably the time to enter or leave the river is from about 1 hour after LW, depending on draft, when there should be sufficient water over the bar and the worst of the shingle banks will still be uncovered.

While waiting for the flood a safe anchorage may be found inshore just S of the Martello Tower at Shingle Street, provided the wind is somewhere between SW and N.

Given sufficient power (not less than 5 knots), it is safest to leave the river on the early flood, when the tide outside will assist any boat bound south.

Both the flood stream and the ebb continue to run into and out of the river for an hour after the change in Hollesley Bay.

The Entrance

When entering on the flood, a boat will tend to be carried into the river on the tidal stream. At the narrows at North Weir Point there is a shoal patch in mid-river. The deepest water lies slightly to the W of this patch, but the streams are strongest in this vicinity and there is considerable turbulence caused by the streams from and to seaward round N Weir Point meeting the main north/south streams in the river.

Long Reach

From the entrance to Dove Point, two miles to the NE, the river is little more than 100m wide and runs between a featureless steep-to shingle bank to the SE and a somewhat shallow shingle and mud shore backed by a sea wall to the NW. This part of the Ore is known as Long Reach, and there is an average of 6m all along it, although because the tides are so fierce and the holding in shingly mud is not very good, it is not advisable, except in emergency, to bring up below Dove

Point. There is a water ski area in the upper part of Long Reach, below Flybury Point.

At Dove Point the river divides around Havergate Island, one part running along the south and the other along the north side of this narrow island. There is a fairly extensive mud spit running out from Dove Point, which is marked by a Spher buoy.

Havergate Island

Havergate is now an important and well-known bird sanctuary under the control of the Royal Society for the Protection of Birds, and landing is prohibited unless permission has been obtained from the Society.

Main Reach

The most direct route up river to Orford Quay is Main Reach, which passes between the E side of Havergate Island and the attenuated shingle bank that stretches from Orfordness down to North Weir Point. The southern half of Main Reach is known as the Narrows, and here the river is hardly more than half a cable wide, and the tides, particularly the ebb, still run very strongly. At the top of Main Reach the river turns northerly towards Orford, about a mile away, and it is then possible to find good holding ground out of the main tidal stream.

A red spherical buoy is sometimes located in Main Reach at the point where the other arm of the river emerges from the W side of Havergate Island. This other arm first of all turns northerly round Flybury Point, and for about half a mile the reach is known as the Lower Gull; one of the best anchorages for a boat waiting to leave the river. The tides still run strongly in Lower Gull, but the holding is better than anywhere in Long Reach. Another good anchorage is in Abraham's Bosom, off the north side of Havergate Island abreast its narrowest part.

At the top of Lower Gull a fairly large creek known as the Butley River branches off in a north-westerly direction. The main stream at this point turns south-easterly for about half a

Looking up the Butley River from the ferry just below The Cliff

mile and then again turns to the NE into Upper Gull. At the northern end of the Upper Gull the channel turns easterly once more and continues for nearly a mile before uniting with Main Reach between Chantry and Cuckold Points.

On the average there is a greater depth of water through Lower Gull and Upper Gull than through Main Reach.

The Butley River

This river or large creek leaves Lower Gull and at first follows a westerly direction for a quarter of a mile before turning north past Boyton Dock and Butley Ferry. The entrance to the creek is marked by a port-hand withy, and there is good anchorage just inside with about 2m at LWS. Shallow draught boats can sometimes lie afloat as far up as Gedgrave Cliff amid pleasant surroundings.

There is an active oysterage in the upper reaches of the river near the Cliff. The beds or trays may not be marked by withies, but there are courteous notice boards indicating the extent of the layings, so visiting yachtsmen should respond by taking care.

Landing is possible at most states of the tide, either at the semi-derelict Boyton Dock or at the Ferry hards, half a mile further north, where Brian Rogers has built jetties and re-opened a year round ferry service between the Boyton and Orford shores (Telephone 01394 410096). From Gedgrave beach on the E bank it is about two miles to Orford – the nearest source of supplies.

Orford Quay

Above Chantry Point the river widens and deepens a little, having between 8 and 10m up to Orford Quay. Extending from the E bank just below the moorings at Orford there is a mud bank that diverts the channel towards the opposite shore for a short distance. The drying edge of the mud is marked by a perch.

The keep of Orford Castle (90ft) is a conspicuous landmark from anywhere in the river S of Orford, and will have been clearly visible from Lower Gull or Main Reach.

It was in 1165 that Henry II decided to build a castle at Orford and it was then that the original quays were construct-ed for unloading the building materials. The castle was

completed in 1173, just in time to be used in Henry's conflict with his Barons. Orford became a flourishing port, sending wool to the Continent at first and later handling coastal trade in coal and grain until 1939.

The view from the top of the keep well repays the climb, as does the equally impressive panorama from the tower of St Bartholomew's church, which was built around the same time as the castle and where there are some excellent brasses and a pair of stocks.

There are moorings on both sides of the channel for a half a mile above and below Orford Quay. Yachts should not anchor in the fairway near the quay. Landing at the quay itself or at the shingle beach north of it is possible at all states of the tide. The concrete slipway at the quay is used by the landing craft ferry and must not be obstructed. Landing on the opposite shore, that is on the Orfordness side, is prohibited by the National Trust, which now owns Orfordness. Visits to the Ness, by ferry from the quay on Thursday, Friday and Saturday, can be booked in advance in the summer, telephone 01394 450637. It is as wel to remember that the yacht moorings at Orford and at Slaughden Quay are laid with their ground chains athwart the stream.

There are no visitors' moorings at Orford, for temporary use of a mooring, contact the Harbour Master, or Marine Services.

Port Guide: Orford	
Harbourmaster	Ralph Brinkley Tel (01394) 450481
Water	Stand-pipe on the quay
Stores	Shops in market square, EC Wed
Chandlery	Limited stock from Marine Services
	Tel: (01394) 450844 VHF Ch 8
Petrol	Garage in town (3/4 mile)
Diesel	From Marine Services or garage
Crane	On quay contact the harbourmaster
Scrubbing	Near quay
Transport	Buses from market square to Ipswich
	and Woodbridge
Club	Orford Sailing Club
Telephone	In car park
PO	In square

3. The River Alde

Tides: HW Slaughden Quay approx 1hr 15mins after HW at entrance. HW Snape Bridge approx 1 hr after Slaughden.
Range: Slaughden Quay Springs 2.5m Neaps 1.1m
Charts: Admiralty 2693, Stanford No. 6, Imray C28
Hazards: Because of winding gutway, make passage between Slaughden and Snape only on rising tide

Above Orford the river turns easterly for a short way and then, abreast Raydon Point, the direction becomes north-easterly along Pigpail Reach. At Raydon Point a water pipe crosses the river to connect with the lighthouse at Orfordness, and the position of the pipe is marked by notice boards. About one and a quarter miles above Orford, the river becomes the Alde, and turns more northerly with deeper water towards the W bank, although all through Blackstakes Reach and Home Reach up to Slaughden Quay, best water will be found roughly midway between the banks. Several racing marks (spar buoys) are located in midstream along these upper reaches of the Alde. Between Orford and Slaughden the depths vary between 5 and 7m at LW, and the width of the LW channel remains about 200m.

The Aldeburgh Yacht Club with its slipway and pontoons at Slaughden Quay. The Martello Tower CC can be seen in the distance beyond the seawall

Slaughden Quay

Abreast the conspicuous Martello Tower, about a quarter of a mile below Slaughden, the river narrows and shallows for a short distance before deepening again and changing direction abruptly off the quay itself. At this point, the river Alde is separated from the sea only by the sea wall and shingle beach – not much more than 100m in all.

Moorings, administered by the Aldeburgh Yacht Club, are laid athwart the stream, on both sides of the channel at Slaughden Quay and although boats are moored fore and aft, they are so closely packed that it is a problem nowadays for a visitor to find an anchorage near the clubhouse. The best

place to bring up is between the Martello Tower and the clubhouse on the E side of the river; this particular Tower, known as 'CC', was the northernmost of the chain that stretched round from the south coast and it is completely different from all the others, being quadrafoil in shape.

Before leaving a boat, either contact the yacht club, or seek the advice of Cruising Association Boatman, Russell Upson, at Upson's boatyard (Tel: 01728 453047).

When you have either anchored or moored, there is clean

This picture shows how closely the river Alde approaches the North Sea on its way down from Snape

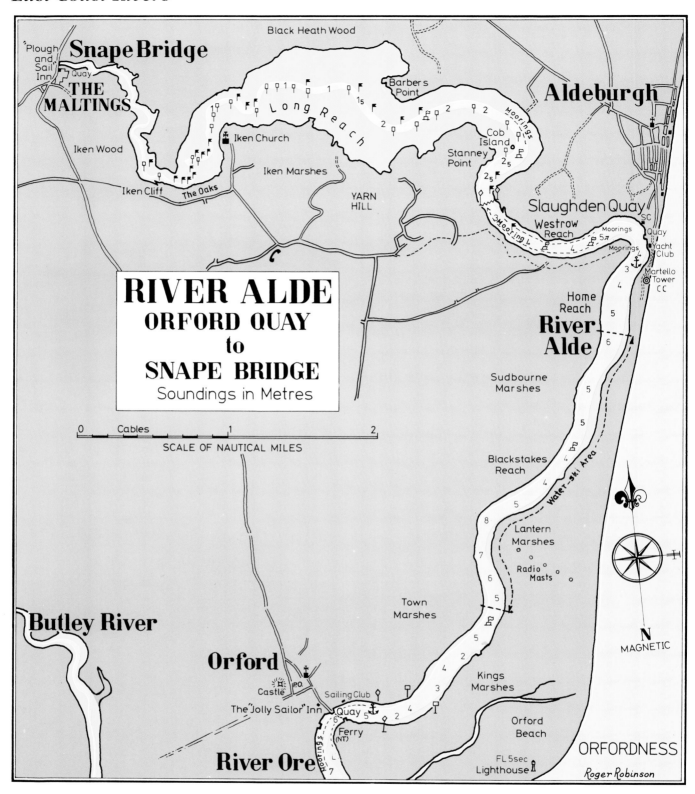

RIVER ALDE
ORFORD QUAY
to
SNAPE BRIDGE
Soundings in Metres

SCALE OF NAUTICAL MILES

landing at the quay near Upson's, on the shingle next to it, or on the slip at the yacht club. Aldeburgh Boatyard, about a quarter of a mile from the quay, offers laying-up facilities and chandlery.

Above Slaughden the river changes direction and turns inland in a general westerly direction for the five or six miles to Snape Bridge. The character of the river now begins to change, and while the banks become farther apart, the LW channel becomes narrower. From here on the river is frequently marked by withies, red to port and green or with twiggy branches to starboard.

The marks are necessarily very numerous – there are more than forty in all (maintained by Aldeburgh YC, to whom we owe thanks for undertaking this formidable task) – and as they are not very conspicuous in certain conditions of light, a very careful look-out must be kept to see that none is missed. It is of course helpful to commence a trip to Iken Cliff or Snape Bridge early on the tide so that the tortuous channel can be seen and the marks understood.

Through Westrow Reach and Short Reach there is about 5m in the channel at LW, and a starboard hand beacon marks the edge of mud extending from the N bank. In Short Reach a power cable crosses the river and is marked by the usual triangular topped beacons. At the top of Short Reach the channel turns north-easterly past two starboard hand beacons and a port hand beacon to Stanney Point. A racing buoy is usually located off Stanney Point but in any case a metal beacon marking the site of the now eroded Cob Island, will serve to identify this point in the river. A derelict brick dock and some moorings will be seen over on the E shore, and here the channel turns back to the NW, round a series of three port hand beacons into Colliers Reach. Three beacons to starboard and three beacons to port mark the channel round Barber's Point and into Long Reach. By this time, the LW channel is but a cable wide, with depths of about 2m.

Past Barber's Point, the river, towards HW, widens to nearly a mile between its banks, and while marshland lies to the south, Black Heath Woods reach down to a sandy beach on the north shore at a spot known locally as 'Little Japan'. At the western end of Long Reach a series of four port hand beacons follow the course of the channel to where it turns sharply to the south towards Sandy Point. Then the channel turns northwesterly into Short Reach and south-westerly again into Church Reach – so named because Iken Church stands on a wooded promontory less than a quarter of a mile away. After this the channel turns westerly into Lower Troublesome Reach and S again into Upper Troublesome Reach. All these abrupt twists and turns of the channel are adequately marked, but care must be taken to ensure that the beacons are passed in the correct order and that none of them is missed.

Above the two Troublesome Reaches, the channel closely approaches the shore near a sandy beach above which a group of oak trees grows. This spot, known as 'The Oaks', is

The navigable head of the River Alde at Snape Bridge. On the extreme left can be seen part of the concert hall in the converted maltings buildings

very pleasant, and offers good landing between half-flood and half-ebb. Then comes Cliff Reach, leading up to Iken Cliff itself, where the LW channel again comes to within 20 yards of the shore.

Iken Cliff

There is not much more than 1.5 metres of water at best in the channel abreast Iken Cliff, but the bottom is mud and the spot provides one of the most attractive anchorages on the Alde. There are a few small boat moorings off the Cliff, but no stores are available near here.

Snape Bridge

From Iken Cliff to Snape Bridge is just over a mile, and the channel, which becomes little more than a gutway, winds between mudbanks and virtually dries out at LW. However, it is possible for craft drawing up to 2m to reach the quay alongside the Maltings at Snape Bridge, and there to take the mud if staying for more than an hour or so. The last mile or so is irregularly marked by some port hand cans and starboard perches.

The Maltings concert hall was built in 1967 as a centre for the Aldeburgh Festival, but now it is used throughout the year for many other performances.

There is a nominal charge for overnight mooring alongside the Maltings Quay, the office there can be contacted on (01728) 688303. The Plough and Sail, the Concert Hall restaurant and the Granary Tea Shop offer a variety of meals. There is water on the quayside, but the nearest supplies, plus two more pubs, are at Snape village, about half a mile away.

Port Guide: Slaughden Quay	
Moorings	Aldeburgh YC Tel (01728) 452562 or Russell Upson (01728) 453047
Water	At yacht club or stand-pipe on quay
Stores	Shops in Aldeburgh (1 mile). EC Wed
Fuel	Diesel from Upson's. Petrol in town. Gas from chandlery
Repairs	Upson's Boatyard. Derrick on quay.
Chandlery	At Aldeburgh Boatyard nearby
Transport	Buses from Aldeburgh to Saxmundham (8 miles). Trains from Saxmundham to Ipswich and London
Clubs	Aldeburgh Yacht Club. Slaughden Sailing Club

Iken Church on its wooded promontory overlooking the upper reaches of the Alde

Graham Jones

4. The River Deben

Tides: At entrance. HW Dover +0.25 Range: Springs 3.2m Neaps 1.9m
(HW Woodbridge approx 45mins after HW in entrance)
Charts: Admiralty 2693, Stanford No. 6, Imray Y16
Waypoint: Woodbridge Haven Buoy 51.58.36N 1.24.20E
Hazards: Strong tide and shoals in entrance (Observe leading marks strictly) Shoal formed 1997 near W bank between Felixstowe Ferry SC and Bawdsey Manor. 'Horse' shoal just above Felixstowe Ferry

Inviting a friend to stay with him aboard his schooner, the Scandal, Edward FitzGerald, translator of The Rubaiyat of Omar Khahyyam, wrote: *'I think you would like this Bawdsey, only about a dozen Fishermen's Houses, built where our River runs into the Sea over a foaming Bar, on one side of which is a good sand to Felixstowe and on the other an orange coloured crag Cliff towards Orford Haven; not a single respectable House or Inhabitants or Lodger; no white Cravats, an Inn with scarce a table and chair and only Bread and Cheese to eat, I often lie here with my Boat: I wish you would come and do so.'*

That was a hundred and twenty years ago, but the Ferry Boat Inn remains although you may now have more than bread and cheese to eat should you wish.

For today's yachtsman who keeps his boat in the Medway, the Crouch or the Blackwater, a visit to the Deben must usually be made during the summer holiday cruise. The Woodbridge river, as the Deben is sometimes called, is only about nine miles long, but it is very attractive and nowadays entirely free from commercial traffic.

Perhaps, the thing that comes first to the East Coast yachtsman's mind when he thinks of the Deben is that there is a

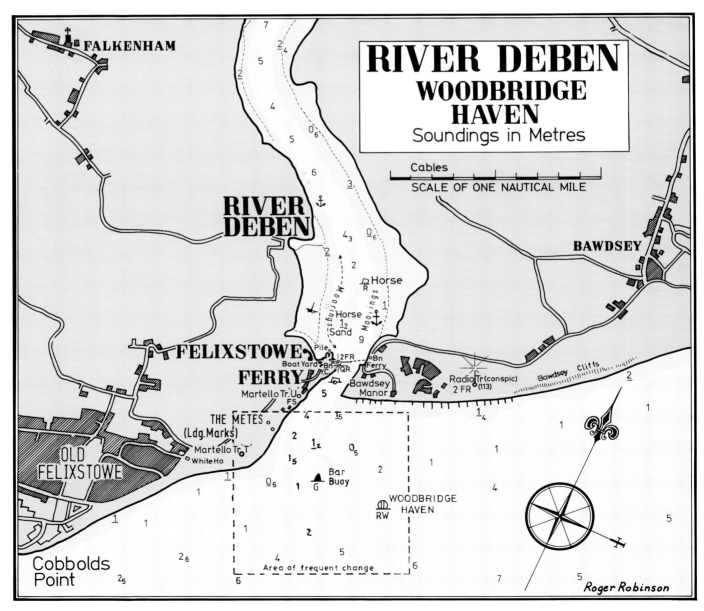

The entrance to the River Deben at LWS, looking south from over the Bawdsey shore. The red can buoy marking the shoal opposite Felixstowe Ferry SC can be seen in the bottom right-hand corner of the picture

shifting shingle bar at the entrance to Woodbridge Haven. This bar ought not to worry anyone unduly because there is a pilot on hand at almost all times during the summer months.

Many more yachts enter and leave the river now than ever before and since most of them hail from Woodbridge, Waldringfield, Ramsholt or Felixstowe Ferry, their skippers usually have the benefit of a local knowledge and so can often act as guide for a newcomer. Nevertheless, when there are no other yachts about and particularly for the first time 'over the bar', it is still a sound idea to take the pilot – Robert Brinkley – who will usually hear a call to 'Late Times' on VHF Channel 8 or come off by prior arrangement. His telephone number is Felixstowe (01394) 270853.

Approaches

Most yachts will approach Woodbridge Haven from the south – often from Harwich harbour, which is only 6 or 7 miles away. A good time to enter the river is about two hours after low water, when there will be a least depth of about 2m over the bar. With so little water to spare, an entrance should never be attempted when there is a bad sea running. But the appearance of the surrounding shoal-water would presumably be enough to scare anyone away on such occasions. A spring ebb can run out of the entrance at 6 knots and any attempt to enter at such times certainly cannot be recommended.

When the approach is from Harwich or from the Wallet, a course should be shaped to pass about half a mile off Felixstowe Pier. When approaching the Deben entrance, most of the details along the low lying shore will be distinguishable – in particular the two Martello Towers (Tower 'T' and Tower 'U'); and the very conspicuous radar pylon (2 FR) just to the north of the entrance to Woodbridge Haven.

Woodbridge Haven buoy is maintained by Trinity House and is spherical with red and white vertical stripes. It is unlit and must never be confused with the green buoy on the bar which is much smaller.

When continuing without a pilot, the Bar buoy must be located before going in. This starboard hand green conical buoy is the only one marking the bar. The precise course from the Bar buoy will depend upon the location of the leading marks or metes.

The 'metes' are both red rectangular boards, the front one bearing a white 'spade' or triangle.

As the shore is neared, the flood will tend to carry a boat in on a course parallel to the beach and about 20 or 30m from it, but there is little risk of approaching the shingle too closely as it is extremely steep-to.

Going in on the flood, the tide will now be pushing really hard, it is necessary to cross towards the Bawdsey shore to leave to port the red can buoy marking a shoal near the Felixstowe Ferry Sailing club. The only obstacle then remaining is the Horse Shoal which occupies the centre of the river immediately above the Felixstowe-Bawdsey Ferry. The Horse Shoal is extensive, and dries out in parts to a height of about 1m. The main channel is to the eastward of the shoal, the channel to port being full of moored craft. It is safer therefore for a stranger to take the main or starboard channel, where there is plenty of water, until the 'Horse' buoy (red can) is reached at the N end of the shoal.

Departure

While it is easier to leave Woodbridge Haven on the ebb tide, this results in any south-bound yacht having to face the remainder of the ebb after leaving the river. It is usually more

A Pandora leaving the River Deben – Martello Tower U at Felixstowe Ferry is left behind and the 'metes' on the fore-shore are beginning to line up to indicate the course for the Bar buoy

Port Guide: Felixstowe Ferry

Pilot	Robert Brinkley Tel (01394) 270853 VHF Ch 8
Water	Standpipe near telegraph beacon and from yard
Stores	Limited supplies from café
Chandler	Near slipway
Repairs	Boatyard and slipway
Fuel	Diesel
Transport	Infrequent bus service to Felixstowe (3 miles)
Telephone	Box near Ferry Boat Inn
Clubs	Felixstowe Ferry Sailing Club Bawdsey Haven Yacht Club

convenient therefore to leave the Haven at about half-flood, depending upon auxiliary power to push a boat over the fast running tidal stream near Felixstowe Ferry. The force of this stream should never be under-estimated, and if an exit is to be made during springs, an auxiliary engine capable of driving the boat at 5 knots will be no more than sufficient unless some help can also be obtained from the sails.

Anchorage

Because of the many moorings between the shoal and the Felixstowe shore, the safest place to bring up to an anchor is above these moorings on the western side of the river where it is easy enough to find good holding ground in a fathom or two at low water. With this anchorage there is the problem of being nearly half a mile from the landing near the Ferry.

An alternative anchorage on the E side can sometimes be found just north of the telegraph cable that crosses the river just above the Ferry and which is marked by conspicuous red and white triangular topmarked beacons on either shore. The attraction of this spot is its close proximity to the convenient steep-to shingle beach on the Felixstowe shore, where one can land from a dinghy at all states of the tide. When bringing up hereabouts, special care must be taken to avoid the nearby moorings, which are laid athwart the stream. Also, it is essential to have ample scope of cable out because of the great strength of the tide – sometimes amounting to 5 knots. So take care when crossing to the other side by dinghy.

RAF Bawdsey, on the north shore opposite Felixstowe Ferry, is now closed and a sailing club, the Bawdsey Haven Yacht Club, is at the former RAF sailing association clubhouse and slipway. Haul out, storage and repair facilities for small

boats is available from the Bawdsey Estate, telephone (01394) 410415. A foot passenger ferry service between Bawdsey and Felixstowe Ferry operates on demand at weekends and during school holidays from Easter to September.

For a mile or two above Felixstowe Ferry the Deben looks very much like a river in Essex rather than Suffolk – with low-lying mudbanks and saltings bordered by a sea wall. The channel, which in its centre has no less than 6m at low water, runs rather closer to the west bank up as far as Ramsholt Reach, where a somewhat abrupt change of scenery occurs.

Ramsholt

On the east bank the land rises sharply to form a modest cliff topped by a pleasant group of pine trees. Nestling under the cliff, close to the old barge quay, is an inn, the Ramsholt Arms, and there are few places more attractive than this on any of the East Coast rivers.

In recent years the moorings at Ramsholt, like everywhere else, have multiplied, but fortunately there is room to anchor in mid-channel if there is no vacant buoy. The harbourmaster, George Collins, usually to be found near the quay or on his yacht *Brio*, will advise on the availability of moorings.

Apart from the Ramsholt Arms, a public telephone, and a post box, there are no facilities at Ramsholt.

Continuing up-river from Kirton Creek, the channel closely

The Deben just above Ramsholt, where the church has an unusual oval tower, and is set in a typical Suffolk backdrop of stubble fields and pine trees

18

The moorings at Ramsholt – there is an attractive landing beneath the Ramsholt Arms and the red crag hill which can be seen in the background

approaches the west bank for a while and then crosses to the east side abreast Ramsholt Woods. There is a very pleasant landing here beneath the trees on a sandy beach known locally as 'The Rocks', so called because of a layer of sandstone rock on the river bed. There are no roads nearby, but on a fine day there is sometimes a 'traffic jam' of yachts! Yachtsmen are asked to refrain from cutting wood to make fires on the beach, or there will soon be no trees left.

At the top of the Rocks Reach, opposite Shottisham Creek, is the first of the up-river marks, which continue as buoys or beacons all the way up to Woodbridge. The first two can buoys, 2 and 2a, and all subsequent port hand buoys are numbered evenly, while those on the starboard hand are odd-numbered.

The next two red cans (4 and 6) mark the mud that stretches out from the west bank at this bend of the river. Just above these buoys there is a patch of shallow water over a 'horse', carrying as little as 1m at LWS. Above No 6 buoy the channel turns NW.

A conical green buoy (No 1) is the first to be left to starboard and it marks the downstream end of an extensive tidal island lying between Waldringfield and Stonner Point. At or near high water there is about 1.5m of water between the east bank and the island, but any boat using this route should proceed cautiously and take frequent soundings past Stonner Point. The two ends of this shallow short cut are marked by beacons.

Waldringfield

The main channel runs to the west of the island, between two lines of moorings and past a green conical buoy, (No.1A). A gap is left in the moorings opposite the beach, off the Waldringfield Sailing Club, so that a limited number of visiting yachts can anchor there. But when this space is taken up and the fairway opposite the beach is likely to become congested, or racing is in progress, it will be better to move either up or down-river to anchor with more space, preferably on the west side of the channel.

Clean landing from a dinghy is possible along the shingle foreshore at almost any time and the Maybush Inn offers splendid views up and down the river.

Continuing up-river from Waldringfield the channel becomes narrower and the mud flats proportionately wider, so that special care must be taken between half-flood and half-ebb, when the mud is only just covered.

No 3 buoy, conical green, marks the northern end of the tidal island, and having left this mark to starboard after passing Waldringfield, the next two red can buoys (Nos 8 and 10) mark an extensive spit off the W bank.

Under Ham Woods there is a low cliff and sandy beach which just invites a picnic – but beware! At high water the beach is hard and sandy, but this hard bottom only extends for a limited distance, after which it abruptly changes to soft mud about a metre deep. If a landing is to be made at 'The Tips', one should return to the dinghy before the mud is uncovered; which happens quickly, for the shore is quite flat hereabouts.

The sandy shore at 'The Tips' resulted from an attempt at the end of the last century by Robert Cobbold to reclaim 150 acres of land from the river. The attempt was stopped by Trinity House, who felt that the scheme would alter the course of the river and interfere with its navigation.

After leaving No 8 and No 10 buoys to port, a green buoy (No 5) is left to starboard below Methersgate Quay, then follows No 12, a red buoy to be left to port opposite the quay.

There are moorings pretty well all the way up from Methersgate Quay to Woodbridge and for the most part they indicate the direction of best water, but additionally there is a closely spaced sequence of channel buoys to guide newcomers through the twists and turns of the Troublesome Reaches.

All the navigational and mooring buoys between Methersgate and Woodbridge are under the control of the Kyson Fairways Committee, who decided to name the channel buoys according to the reaches in which they are located. So we now have buoys with names such as: 'Upper Troublesome', 'Lower Troublesome', 'Granary Reach' and 'Crummy Moore'.

There are drying moorings and pontoons with water and power at the boatyard on the S side of Martlesham Creek.

One more spherical green (No 13) and one more red (No 16) buoy mark the way to the line of moorings extending down-river from Woodbridge.

Four more port hand (red can) buoys (Nos 18 to 24) mark the channel between Eversons shed and the entrance to the Tide Mill Yacht Harbour, and are helpful because deeper water changes from side to side of the river hereabouts.

Loders' Cut

Towards the end of the last century a channel was cut to avoid the bend past Kyson Quay. The purpose of Loders' Cut, as the channel is called, was to revive Woodbridge's failing maritime trade. The plan was not very successful, although the cut remains and can be safely used by light draught boats for about 1½ to 2 hours either side of high water. There are port and starboard hand marks at both ends of the cut, which now has the same water as in the main channel.

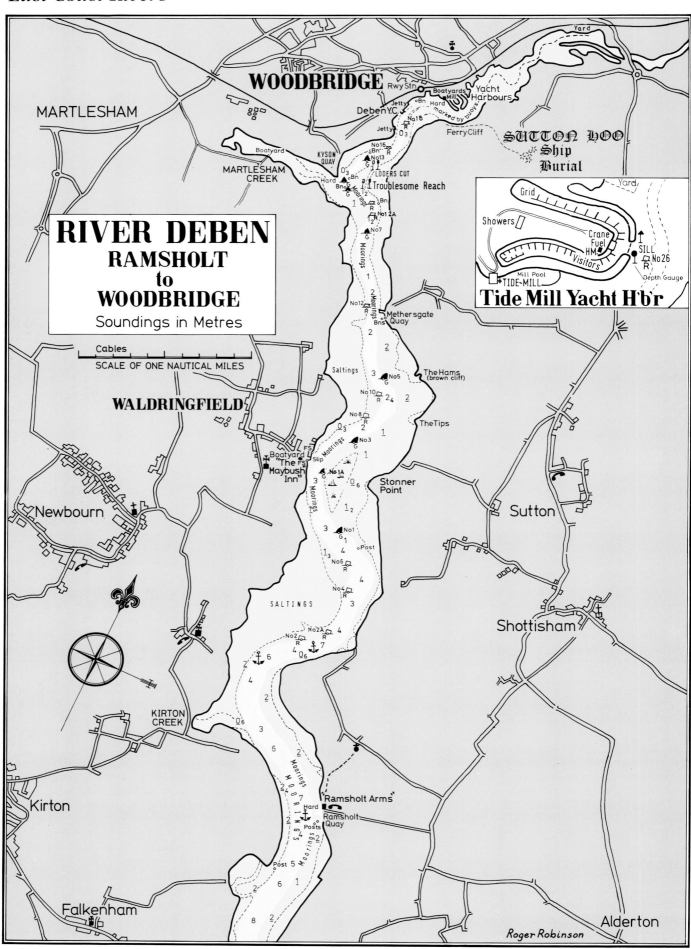

MARTLESHAM

WOODBRIDGE

Rwy Stn
Boatyards
Mill
Yacht
Harbours
Deben Y.C.
Jetty
Bn
Hard
marked by buoys
Jetty
No18
O3
FerryCliff
SUTTON HOO
Ship
Burial

No16
G
No13
Boatyard
KYSON
QUAY
O3
Bn
Hard
LODERS CUT
Troublesome Reach
Bn
1
No1 ZA
R
No7

MARTLESHAM
CREEK

RIVER DEBEN
RAMSHOLT
to
WOODBRIDGE
Soundings in Metres

Cables
SCALE OF ONE NAUTICAL MILES

WALDRINGFIELD

No12
R
Moorings
Mothersgate
Bns
Quay
2

2

Saltings
3
No5
G
The Hams
(brown cliff)
No10
R
2 4
2
No8
R
2
The Tips
O3
No3
G
1
Moorings
Slip
FS
Boatyard
"The
Maybush
Inn"
No1A
G
3
O6
Stonner
Point

Newbourn

Moorings
1 2

3
No1
G
Post
1 3
4
No6
R
4
No4
R

Sutton

Shottisham

SALTINGS
3

No2A
4
No2
R
4 7
4
O6

Kirton

KIRTON
CREEK
3
O6

2

Moorings
2
O7

Moorings
Hard
Posts
"Ramsholt Arms"
Ramsholt
Quay

2

2

Post 5
2
6
1

Falkenham

8
2

Alderton

Roger Robinson

Tide Mill Yacht H'br

Yard
Grid
Showers
Crane
Fuel
HM
SILL
No26
R
Visitors
Mill Pool
TIDE-MILL
Depth Gauge

On the approach to Woodbridge, the lines of moorings extend well downriver from the town, and most boats take the ground at low water

Woodbridge

There are moorings on both sides of the channel at Woodbridge, but most of the boats take the ground at low water. A few deeper draught craft are located in 'holes' where there is more water; one of these being in midstream abreast of Everson's old building shed, quite close to the re-built bandstand on the sea wall promenade.

But generally, a visiting yacht must expect to come and go on a tide or else be prepared to ground for a while at low water. It is high water at Woodbridge 45 minutes later than at Felixstowe Ferry.

When staying at Woodbridge for a few hours in order to see the town and obtain stores the best place to bring up is

between the moorings just above the clubhouse of the Deben Yacht Club, which was established in 1838. From here, it is easy to land at Everson's wooden jetty, or a cable further up, at Ferry Quay.

The old ferry dock is fitted out as a yacht harbour. Although it dries out at LW, there are stagings to lie to and the mud is soft.

Further upstream the old tide mill pool has been excavated to form a horseshoe-shaped yacht basin, where yachts can lie afloat at all states of the tide. The Tide Mill Yacht Harbour has a sill over which boats drawing 2m can pass at HW neaps and those drawing as much as 3m at the top of a good spring tide. However craft drawing more than 1.5m (5ft) should not attempt entry after HW on a neap tide. Buoys for waiting yachts are placed just outside the entrance.

There has been a tide mill where the present Woodbridge Mill stands since 1170 and, thanks to an energetic Preservation Society, this last remaining tide mill on the East Coast can be seen in operation.

There are three yards above the mill; the first is Roberton's with a slipway and a travel lift. The Granary Yacht Harbour at Dock Lane, Melton, is about a mile above the mill and they will send you a sketch chart showing the buoyed channel up to their pontoon berths. Larkman's yard at Melton wharf uses its 9 ton crane mainly for lifting boats out for their winter lay-up.

You can take the tide above Woodbridge to Wilford Bridge. Such an excursion is well worth while if it includes a walk from Wilford Bridge to see the site of the Saxon burial ship at Sutton Hoo, the discovery of which, in 1939, has been described as *'the most marvellous find in the archaeological annals of England'.* It is also possible to land at Sutton Ferry Cliff opposite the marina entrance, and follow the footpath to the site.

Port Guide: Woodbridge	
Tide Mill Yacht Harbour	Tel (01394) 385745 comprehensive facilities include showers, toilets, water, fuel, etc
Water	Tap on Ferry Quay
Stores	Many shops in town. EC Wed
Petrol and oil	Petrol from garages in town. Diesel and gas from all yards
Chandlers	At Lime Kiln Quay and Dock Lane, Melton
Chart Agents	SCD Ltd corner of Quayside and Quay Street
Repairs	Several yards, slipways and cranes. Sailmaker near Yacht Harbour
Telephone	Box in station yard
Transport	Train service to Ipswich, then to London. Buses to Ipswich
Clubs	Deben Yacht Club, Woodbridge Cruising Club

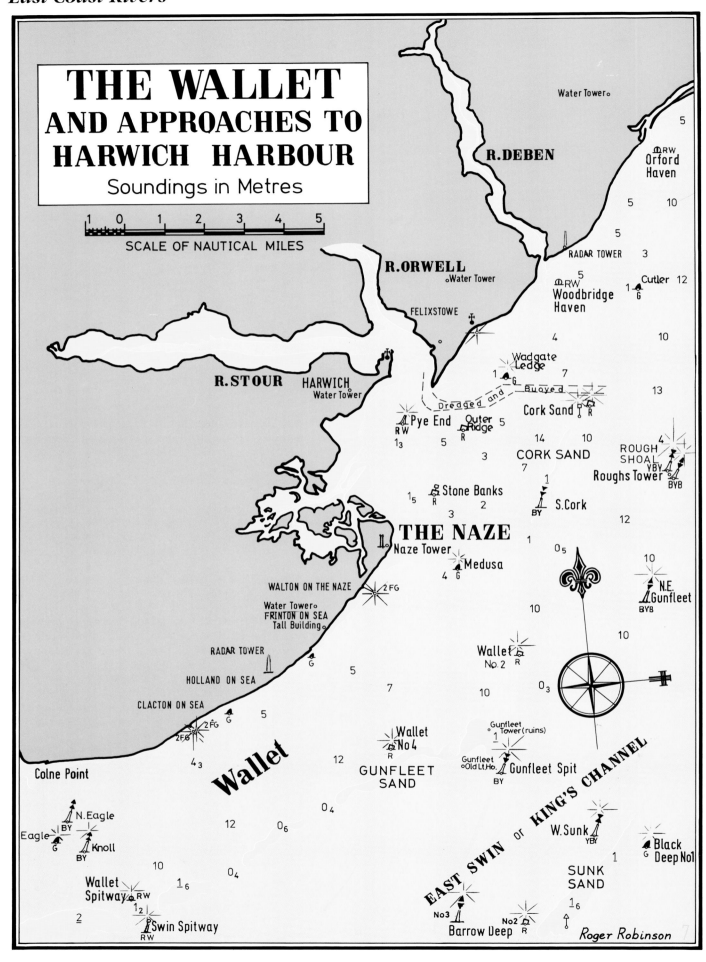

THE WALLET
AND APPROACHES TO
HARWICH HARBOUR
Soundings in Metres

SCALE OF NAUTICAL MILES

R.DEBEN

Water Tower

Orford Haven

RADAR TOWER

R.ORWELL
Water Tower

FELIXSTOWE

Woodbridge Haven

Cutler

Wadgate Ledge

Buoyed

Cork Sand

R.STOUR   HARWICH
Water Tower

Dredged and

Pye End
RW

Outer Ridge

CORK SAND

ROUGH SHOAL

Roughs Tower

Stone Banks

S.Cork

THE NAZE

Naze Tower

Medusa

WALTON ON THE NAZE

2 FG

N.E. Gunfleet

Water Tower
FRINTON ON SEA
Tall Building

RADAR TOWER

Wallet No.2

HOLLAND ON SEA

CLACTON ON SEA

2 FG
2FG

Wallet
No 4

GUNFLEET SAND

Gunfleet Tower (ruins)

Gunfleet Old Lt.Ho.   Gunfleet Spit

Colne Point

Wallet

W.Sunk

N.Eagle

Eagle

Knoll

Black Deep No1

SUNK SAND

Wallet Spitway

Swin Spitway

EAST SWIN or KING'S CHANNEL

No3   No2

Barrow Deep

Roger Robinson

5. Harwich Harbour

Tides: HW Dover +0.50 Range: Springs 3.6m Neaps 2.3m
Charts: Admiralty 1491, Stanford No 6, Imray Y16
Waypoints: Pitching Ground Buoy 51.55.39N 1.21.16E. Landguard Buoy 51.55.35N 1.18.98E.
                Cliff Foot Buoy 51.55.69N 1.18.64E. S Shelf Buoy 51.56.17N 1.18.67E. Guard Buoy 51.57.03N 1.17.88E.
                Shotley Spit Buoy 51.57.26N 1.17.67E
Hazards: Shipping entering and leaving (Keep clear of dredged channel)

The earliest indirect reference to a harbour at Harwich is to be found in the Anglo-Saxon Chronicle for the year 885: *'The same year sent King Alfred a fleet from Kent into East Anglia. As soon as they came to Stourmouth there met them sixteen ships of the pirates and they fought with them, took all ships and slew the men. As they returned homeward with their booty they met a large fleet of pirates and fought with them the same day, but the Danes had the victory.'*

Some people believe that Bloody Point off Shotley owes its name to the first of these two battles, fought more than a thousand years ago.

Nowhere else on the East Coast is there an expanse of protected deep water as extensive as that formed at the junction of the rivers Orwell and Stour, which emerge to the sea as one between Beacon Cliff and Landguard Point.

The Haven Ports, comprising Felixstowe, Harwich and Ipswich, between them now handle so much traffic that there are approximately 24,000 commercial movements annually, day and night. With the deeper dredged channel now open, some of the world's largest container ships use it and small boat sailors must therefore stay well clear of the channel whenever possible.

The buoyage and marking of Harwich Harbour and the River Stour are the responsibility of the Harwich Haven Authority.

Approaches

From the S or SE the harbour can be approached in small craft by two routes, both avoiding the many shoals and banks that lie off the entrance. The course from the S, through the Medusa Channel, is described under 'Approaches to Walton Backwaters' and the same directions will serve until the Landguard Buoy (BY N Card Q) is in sight.

Another way into Harwich Harbour from the SE is through a channel known as the Gullet, passing about midway between the Medusa (Con G Fl G 5s) and the S Cork (S Card) and leaving the unlit Stonebanks (Can R) to port.

From the E the main deep water channel is exceptionally well marked by pairs of buoys, starting with the Shipway (S Card) and Cross (Y Pillar) buoys out beyond the Cork Sand.

Because of the big ship traffic, a yacht should keep to a track south of the well marked dredged channel.

When approaching Harwich Harbour from the Deben or the Alde, the deep water channel must be crossed as quickly as possible to keep away from the berths at the Port of

A yacht outward bound from Harwich Harbour, passing the historic Harwich skyline – the old light tower is one of a pair of leading marks built in the time of Charles II

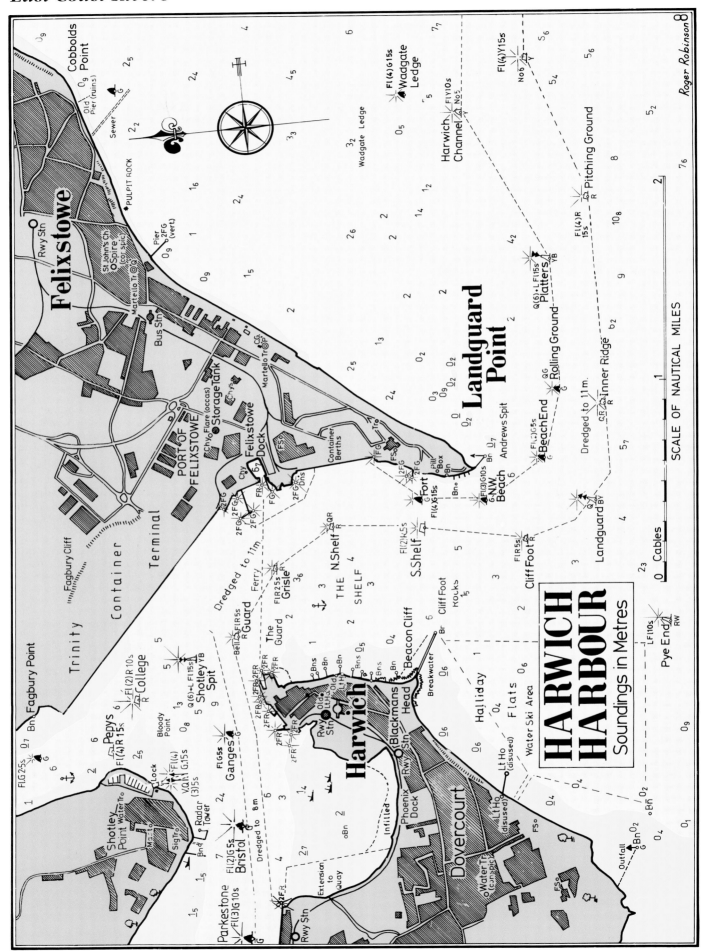

HARWICH HARBOUR
Soundings in Metres

Roger Robinson 8

24

Harwich, showing the old town, the new quays and the old Pound. Beyond, further up the River Stour, is Parkeston Quay with a Stena Line fast sea cat about to leave the terminal

Felixstowe. The recommended crossing point is from between the Platters (S Card) buoy and the Rolling Ground (G) buoy, to a point between the Pitching Ground (R) buoy and the Inner Ridge (R) buoy.

When approaching from the E it is best for yachts to keep to the S of the dredged channel, past the Cork Sand, Pitching Ground and Inner Ridge buoys, before turning to the N, leaving the Landguard and Cliff Foot buoys to starboard.

The old disused leading light towers on the Harwich shore, built in the time of Charles II and still standing, no longer serve as aids to navigation, but the lower one now houses a maritime museum.

The Harbour is entered between Beacon Cliff breakwater to the W and Landguard Point to the E. The width of the entrance is rather less than a mile including the water over the Cliff Foot Rocks, located 1½-3 cables off the end of the breakwater. These rocks have as little as 2m over them at LWS and, when

entering the Harbour from Dovercourt Bay, they can be avoided by passing within a cable of the beacon on the end of the breakwater. Whenever the latter course is taken it is important to continue in a north-easterly direction over towards the Felixstowe shore after clearing the breakwater. Any temptation to turn to the N across the Guard shoal must be resisted until a position has been reached about midway between the Harwich and Felixstowe shores, near the N Shelf red can buoy. The Guard shoal has no more than a metre over it in patches at LWS.

The E or Felixstowe shore is entirely given over to container docks that are in constant use; ferries, including a fast Sea Cat, operate frequently from Parkeston Quay. It is therefore prudent to keep a very sharp lookout for movement of ships or ferries berthing or leaving the port, and to keep to the recommended yacht track on the Harwich side.

Harbour Operations frequency, Channel 71, is extremely busy at all times and yachtsmen are asked not to use it. However, it is useful to monitor that frequency in order to anticipate the movements of shipping. On weekends during summer months the Harbour Patrol Launch will provide assistance and advice to yachtsmen and maintains a listening watch on VHF Ch 11.

Anchorages

There are several areas within which anchoring is always prohibited because of the necessity to maintain a clear passage for the heavy traffic to and from Ipswich, Parkeston Quay, Harwich and Felixstowe. The principal areas prohibited are:
(1) Anywhere in the fairway or within 200ft thereof between Parkeston Quay and the Rolling Ground buoy.
(2) Between the western edge of the dredged channel and a line joining the Guard and N Shelf buoys.

Harwich/Angel Pound

It is possible for small yachts, drawing no more than a metre or so, to lie afloat for a while around the high water period, alongside Harwich Quay, together with the local fishing craft. This area is very busy and susceptible to wash from passing

Port Guide: Harwich	
Harbourmaster	Tel: (01255) 243030
Harbour Operations	243000 VHF Ch 71
Harbour Patrol Launch	VHF Ch 11
Water	Town pier or from Trinity House Buoy Yard, by courtesy of Trinity House
Stores	Shops in town EC Wed
Fuel	Some distance away
Repairs	Chandlery and sailmaker in town
Transport	Good train service to London. Buses from quayside to Colchester, Manningtree, Walton-on-the-Naze. Coach service to London.
Water Taxi service	Parkeston to Shotley and the Orwell Tel: 0589 371138 (mobile) 01472 787567 or VHF Ch 37.
Clubs	Harwich and Dovercourt Sailing Club. Harwich Town Sailing Club

An aerial view of Shotley Point Marina with, in the distance, the extended Trinity Container Terminal at Felixstowe on the east bank of the River Orwell

commercial vessels to and from Parkeston Quay. Berths alongside the railway or W pier will usually be occupied by Trinity House servicing ships. There are landing steps at both corners of the Pound.

Landing is possible at most states of the tide at a quay to the S of Train Ferry Pier, in Gas House Creek. This is where some of the local fishing boats berth.

Much of the large expanse of drying mud known as Bathside Bay, to the W of Harwich and N of Dovercourt, has been filled in for the extension of Parkeston Quay. This project, together with a dredging programme to increase LW depths in the channel, means that there are more ships in the entrance to the Stour, and some of them are larger than we have seen up to now.

Shotley

On the north shore at Shotley there is good anchorage except in strong southerly or westerly winds. Probably the best spot to choose is inside the trot of moorings situated about two cables SE of Shotley Pier. Three or four metres with a mud bottom is easy to find here, within a short distance from both the hard and the pier.

The Ganges training base is no more. Only the flagstaff remains to remind us that once a year some brave cadet would stand proudly atop its cap.

Shotley Point Marina

To reach the marina from Shotley Spit S Cardinal buoy, a yacht should proceed parallel to the deep water channel into the River Stour, passing close N of the conical green Ganges buoy to the beacons marking the outer end of the dredged channel leading to the marina lock-gates. The beacons are lit; Q (3) 5s to Port and Fl (4) G 15s to Starboard.

A special form of indicating signal has been installed at the

Shotley marina to facilitate keeping to the dredged channel leading to the lock (which is manned 24 hours a day). The INOGON system, as it is called, depends upon the 'passive interaction between the helmsman's line of vision and a mosaic pattern produced by the leading mark.' The practical result is that when a yacht is on the correct bearing, a vertical black line will be seen down the middle of the screen, while any deviation from the correct course will cause the moire pattern to form arrows indicating whether course should be changed to port or to starboard. the density of the arrow pattern will indicate how great the correction should be. There are waiting pontoons on the port-hand just outside the lock.

Felixstowe Dock

When, in 1886, Col Tomline dug out a dock at the end of his private railway, he could never have dreamt of the port of Felixstowe as it is today.

The container terminal at Felixstowe now extends up river almost as far as Fagbury Point and the original Dock is no longer suitable for yachts, even as a temporary berth; anchoring in the vicinity is strictly prohibited. (Gone are the days of *Goblin* in *We Didn't Mean to Go to Sea.*)

Port Guide: Shotley Point Marina	
Telephone	(01473) 788982 VHF Ch 80, 37
Water	On pontoons
Fuel	Diesel just inside marina
Gas	At chandlery
Stores	Adjacent
Repairs	Full range of services, 30 ton travel-lift
	10 ton crane
Chandler	On site
Transport	Bus service from Shotley to Ipswich
Club	Open to visitors

6. The River Orwell

Tides: HW Dover + 0100 Range: Springs 3.7m Neaps 2.3m. HW Ipwich approx 15mins after Pin Mill
Charts: Admiralty 2693, Stanford No 6, Imray Y16
Waypoints: Pepys 51.57.71N 01.17.00E, College Buoy 51.57.52N 01.17.44E, Orwell No. 1 Buoy 51.58.25N 01.16.77E
Hazard: Large ships in narrow dredged channel

In his book Orwell Estuary, W G Arnott comments on the unchanging nature of much of the river: *'One wonders that the river and its surroundings remain so unspoilt and have suffered so little from the overspill of Ipswich. For this we have largely to thank the much maligned landowners of the estates along its banks. These estates represented a system for which some will say there is little moral justification, but…in the case of the Orwell (it) has saved its banks from spoilation.'*

The Orwell extends for about nine miles in a general north-westerly direction from the northern side of Harwich Harbour up to the docks at Ipswich. Commercial traffic uses the river, and some of it is surprisingly large. For the benefit of these big ships a dredged and well-buoyed channel is provided by the Ipswich Port Authority.

On leaving Harwich Harbour, the entrance to the Orwell lies between Shotley Point to the W, and the northern extension of Felixstowe's deep-water quays to the E. The two channel marks indicating the entrance are Shotley Spit Buoy (S Card YB Q (6)+L Fl 15s) and the red can College buoy (Fl(2)10s) on the west bank opposite the Trinity container terminal. Some ships using the northern berths of the terminal are unable to turn off the berth and have to manoeuvre stern first to or from the swinging area E of Shotley Spit and Guard buoys.

There is an average depth of 7.5 metres in the main channel, for a width of about two cables, although at HW, with the mud all covered, the width from bank to bank is almost a mile.

When entering the Orwell from the Stour it is not necessary to round Shotley Spit buoy, which can be safely left a cable or so to starboard.

East Shotley Anchorage

There is a useful anchorage just inside the river and on the W shore, roughly NE of E Shotley Martello Tower (now topped by a large green water tank). This spot is known as Stone Heaps, and there is something of a hard on which to land, and a footpath that can be followed via the sea wall and past the marina into the village at Shotley Gate.

Even today a barge or two may be brought up, waiting a tide at Stone Heaps. The holding in mud is good, but care must be taken to anchor out of the channel and yet in enough water to remain afloat. This is not always as easy as it seems, as the edge of the channel is quite steep-to. A riding light is essential.

The red can lit buoys Pepys and College, up river of Shotley Point Marina and the green conical buoy (Fl G 2.5s) off Fagbury Point are maintained by the Harwich Harbour Authority, but all of the other buoys in the Orwell are the responsibility of the Ipswich Port Authority. The first pair of their buoys are the 'Orwell', (Red can F1R 2.5s) and the No.1, (Con G F1G 5s). A telegraph cable crosses the river between Fagbury Point and the Shotley shore, its precise position being indicated by red and white beacons with diamond-shaped topmarks. Other cables cross the river farther up, and all are marked in the same way, with a beacon on each shore.

Looking across the River Orwell at Collimer Point towards the Suffolk Yacht Harbour on the east bank near Levington

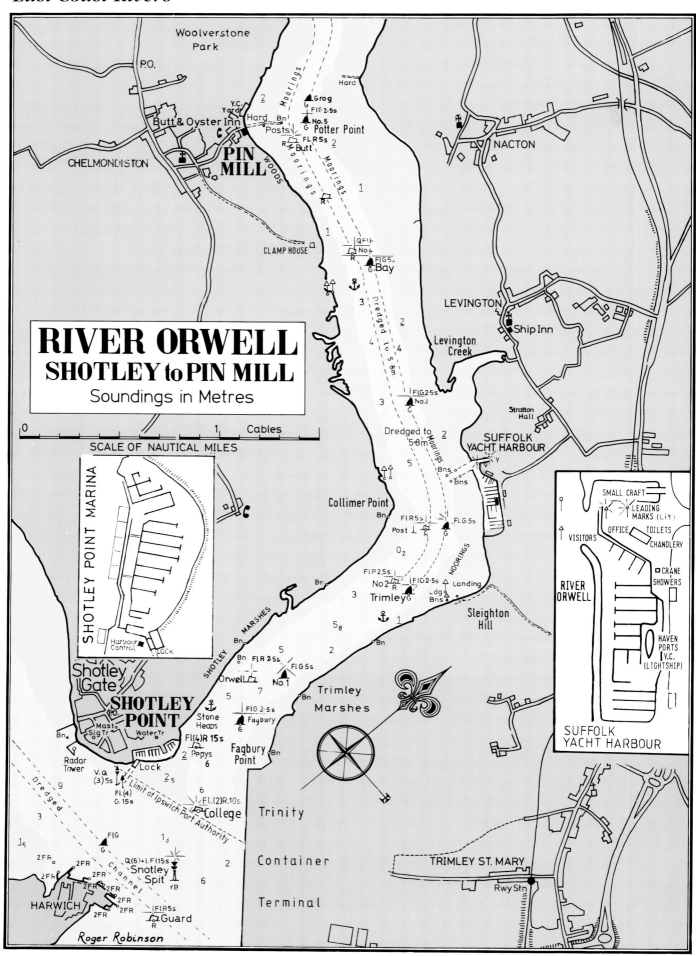

RIVER ORWELL
SHOTLEY to PIN MILL
Soundings in Metres

Once inside the entrance to the Suffolk Yacht Harbour, a sharp turn to starboard is made, then the rows of pontoons come into sight on the port-hand side

Above Fagbury Point the river follows a northerly direction through Lower Reach to Collimer Point. There is low, marshy ground on either side of Lower Reach, but behind the marshes there are hills which close in on the river abreast Collimer Point. A little below the Point is a pair of buoys marking the width of the channel that is dredged to 6m all the way up to Ipswich. The starboard-hand green conical buoy of the pair is marked 'Trimley' and it flashes green every 2.5 seconds. Abreast Collimer Point itself there is a second pair of buoys – both of them lit. There is also a tide gauge on the Point, and inshore of that are the remains of another of the hards that once were in regular use along both banks of the river. On the opposite shore it is also possible to land fairly conveniently just S of a small area of saltings below Sleighton Hill. There are a few small boat moorings nearby.

After rounding Collimer Point and entering Long Reach, the direction of the river becomes north-westerly, and the true character of the Orwell is revealed.

Just above Collimer Point, on the N side of the river, is the Suffolk Yacht Harbour at Stratton Hall, near Levington Creek. The entrance to the harbour is a dredged channel about 30m wide, holding some 1.5m of water at LW neaps.

The entrance channel is marked at its outer end by a spherical orange buoy and then by port and starboard poles with topmarks. There are leading lights at night. (Outer Iso Y 1s and Inner Oc Y 3s + 1s).

Port Guide: Suffolk Yacht Harbour
Tel: (01473) 659465 VHF Ch 80 and 37 M (Daylight hours)

Water	Near entrance. All pontoons
Fuel	Petrol and Diesel oil from pumps near entrance, gas from chandler
Stores	Provisions and off-licence on site
Repairs	Shipwrights, sailmaker and engineers on site. Travel lift, slipway and scrubbing posts
Chandler	Store on site
Telephone	Available
Transport	Buses Felixstowe and Ipswich (1 mile walk) Local taxi service
Club	Haven Ports YC aboard LV87 has bar and restaurant

Visitors can, if there is space, temporarily leave their yachts at a pontoon just inside and opposite the entrance, while reporting to the harbourmaster for instructions. The harbour has been extended over the years and now provides permanent and visitors' pontoon berths with power and water; focal point is the Haven Ports Yacht Club HQ on the old light vessel no.87.

Deep draught boats, unsure of the entrance, can sometimes find a mooring free immediately up-river of the entrance buoy.

The next buoy, No 3 (Con G Fl G 2.5s), and a few yacht moorings lie off the entrance to Levington Creek marked by withies. This little drying gutway was once regularly used by trading barges, and it is still possible to sound a way up to the old wharf at the head of the creek. From the wharf it is only a short walk to the hamlet of Levington and the Ship Inn.

Between Levington and Potter Point there is another pair of lit buoys – 'The Bay' is conical green with a flashing green 5s light while its opposite – a red can buoy No 4 – has a quick flashing red light.

There is the possibility of anchoring on the S side, just below No 4 buoy and opposite Clamp House, where there will be shelter from the SW and landing is possible.

Pin Mill

For the East Coast cruising man, the Orwell means Pin Mill and it is this unique hamlet, with its waterside inn and the prospect of a collection of spritties on the hard, that brings us back time and time again.

If it is at all possible it is preferable to find a mooring rather than drop an anchor at Pin Mill. Quite often there are one or two moorings available for visitors, just below the hard. The harbourmaster will usually know when a mooring is free.

If an anchorage has to be found, it is better to be below the moorings and well clear of the dredged channel, because ships approach the Pin Mill moorings very closely as they round No 5 buoy at Potter Point. The holding, in mud, is good, while protection is almost complete. Only in the case of strong north-westerly winds will a boat be disturbed, except by the sometimes considerable wash from passing freighters or tankers.

The very long hard at Pin Mill is not long enough to provide landing at low water springs. You may have to wait an hour or more to avoid the mud. When the tide is rising it

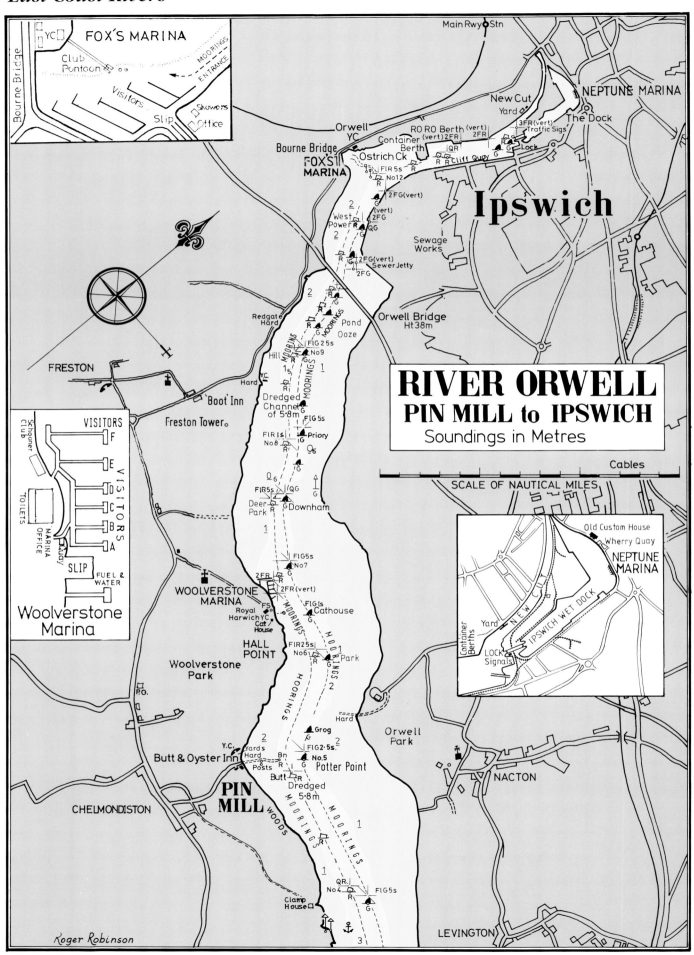

FOX'S MARINA

YC

Club Pontoon

MOORINGS
ENTRANCE

Visitors

Slip

Showers
Office

Bourne Bridge

Main Rwy Stn

NEPTUNE MARINA

New Cut
Yard

The Dock

3FR(vert)
Traffic Sigs

Orwell YC

Bourne Bridge

FOX'S
MARINA

Ostrich Ck

RO RO Berth (vert)
(vert) 2FR
2FR

Container
Berth

QR

R R Cliff Quay

R G Lock

G

Ipswich

FIR 5s
No12

R

2FG(vert)

West
Power

R
(vert)
2FG
QG

2FG(vert)

R

G Sewer Jetty

2FG

Sewage
Works

Orwell Bridge
Ht 38m

Redgate
Hard

MOORINGS

MOORINGS

Pond
Ooze

RIVER ORWELL
PIN MILL to IPSWICH
Soundings in Metres

Hill

FIG 2 5s
No9

Cables

YC

Hard

R
Ri

SCALE OF NAUTICAL MILES

FRESTON

Dredged
Channel
of 5·8m

FIG 5s

'Boot' Inn

Freston Tower

FIR 1s
No8

G Priory

R

Q 5

G

VISITORS

F

Schooner
Club

FIR5s

IQG

Q 6

Old Custom House

Wherry Quay

E

VISITORS

D

Deer
Park

G Downham

NEPTUNE
MARINA

C

TOILETS

B

MARINA
OFFICE

A

Quay

FIG5s
No7

R

Container
Berths

Yard

NEW CUT

IPSWICH WET DOCK

SLIP

FUEL &
WATER

2FR
R

2FR(vert)

LOCK
Signals

Woolverstone
Marina

WOOLVERSTONE
MARINA

FS

FIG1s
Cathouse

Royal
Harwich YC

Cat
House

MOORINGS

R

HALL
POINT

FIR 2 5s
No6

R

G

Park

Woolverstone
Park

MOORINGS

P.O.

G Grog

Hard

Orwell
Park

Y.C.

Yard

Hard

2

FIG 2·5 s

2

NACTON

Butt & Oyster Inn

Posts

R Bn

G No.5

PIN
MILL

Butt

R

Potter Point

CHELMONDISTON

Dredged
5·8m

WOODS

MOORINGS

1

QR.
No4

R

FIG5s

G

Clamp
House

LEVINGTON

3

Roger Robinson

The Butt and Oyster at the top of the hard, and the wooded foreshore viewed from the Pin Mill Sailing Club

is as well to haul the dinghy well up the gulley formed by the stream running down the side of the hard.

The upper hard at Pin Mill is no half-hearted affair, but a fine expanse of firm shingle on which there are sometimes barges undergoing repair. Scrubbing, too, is made easy by reason of the several stout posts that are available. At the top of the hard is the Butt and Oyster Inn, itself awash at HW springs. The hard continues, almost imperceptibly, straight into a lane that leads up the valley to Chelmondiston.

Chelmondiston

Chelmondiston – 'Chelmo' for short – is about three-quarters of a mile from the hard at Pin Mill, and the walk up the lane seems to belong to Devon rather than Suffolk. There are grocery stores, a butcher's shop, pubs and a PO in this busy little village.

Above Pin Mill the channel turns more northerly into Potter Reach, and about two cables beyond the buoy marking Potter Point, on the eastern shore, is a hard that can be used at most states of the tide to land in Orwell Park. No 6 buoy (R can Fl 2.5s) marks the mud off Hall Point, while a green conical buoy (Fl G 5s) on the other side of the channel is located in Park Bight, together with a continuous line of moorings used by craft based on Woolverstone Marina.

Woolverstone

The dredged channel now approaches the W bank of the river to within a cable, abreast the 'Cat House' buoy (Con G Fl G 1s). There is no room to lie to an anchor. Under no circumstances should a boat anchor inside the buoyed channel, as vessels up to 9,000 tons use the river regularly.

On the S bank there is a short pier and a concrete landing place known as Cat House Hard which belongs to the Woolverstone Marina and is used by their customers as well as members of the Royal Harwich Yacht Club, whose premises and dinghy landing are nearby. The club was formed in 1845 and by 1848 was holding its first 'Eastern Coast Regatta' in

Port Guide: Pin Mill	
Harbourmaster	Tony Ward Tel: (01473) 780276
Water	Tap alongside clubhouse of Pin Mill SC. At Wards's chandlery, near hard
Stores	Shops at Chelmondiston, EC Wed
Fuel	Petrol, diesel and gas at top of hard
Repairs	Boatyard and chandler
Scrubbing post	On hard. (For use, consult HM.)
Transport	Bus service to Ipswich and Shotley from Chelmondiston
Club	Pin Mill Sailing Club
Telephone	In public car park, 100 yards up the lane

Harwich Harbour, where the headquarters of the club remained for the next hundred years. In 1946 the club moved up-river to Woolverstone. The RHYC is always happy to allow visiting yachtsmen to use its facilities, which, during the season, consist of showers, restaurant and a bar. The club has no moorings of its own, as these all belong to the Woolverstone Marina.

There is a pontoon marina taking 200 boats immediately upstream of the pier, just S of the dredged channel, where berths are accessible at all times.

Visitors can berth on the ends of any pontoon or on Pontoon 'F', the last one upstream.

A Marina Master is on duty seven days a week throughout the year.

No 7 buoy (Con G Fl G 5s) together with a red can (Fl R 5s) mark the commencement of Downham Reach and now the dredged channel becomes less than a cable wide so that the buoys must be strictly observed unless it is near HW. Another unlit green conical buoy marks the eastern edge of the channel through Downham Reach; the western edge is indicated first by a lit red can (Fl R 5s) and then by No 8, a red can light buoy (Fl R 5s), abreast the prominent tower in Freston Park. Just above No 8 buoy there is a green conical buoy (Fl G 5s)

Port Guide: Woolverstone Marina

Telephone no.	(01473) 780206
VHF	Chs 80 and 37 M
Water	From end of pier
Diesel fuel	From end of pier
Gas	From Marina Master's office
Repairs	Yard equipped for all services. Slipway. 25-ton mobile crane
Showers and Laundrette	Near pontoons
Chandler	Nearby
Stores	From Pantry at Marina
Clubs	Royal Harwich Yacht Club. 'Schooner' Club
Telephone	Kiosk on hard

called the Priory, on the east side of the channel. The next pair of lit buoys are the Hill (Fl R 5s) and No 9 (Fl G 2.5s).

Along here there are a number of small boat moorings just outside the channel. They belong to the Stoke SC whose clubhouse is just below Freston Tower. From Freston hard it is a short walk up the road to the Boot Inn, where water may be obtained and where buses stop on the Shotley-Ipswich route.

By now the Orwell bridge will dominate the view ahead, but since it provides a clearance of 125ft (38m) and the width between the only navigable span is 300ft (92m) it should inconvenience yachtsmen very little. No ship can hit any of the eight piers that rise from the river bed because their bases are all protected by artificial islands'.

However, the bridge crosses the navigable channel at an angle so that the pilot of any commercial vessel about to pass under it will have his attention fully occupied without having to worry about any nearby yacht. Common sense therefore dictates that whenever possible the yachtsman should avoid being in the vicinity of the bridge if a commercial vessel is passing through.

There is an unlit port hand buoy, No 10, opposite the green conical No 11 buoy very near the bridge where the dredged channel is only about half a cable wide.

A green conical buoy, the E Fen (QG), marks the east side of the channel above the bridge while No 12 Cliff Reach Buoy (Can R Fl R 5s) on the west side also serves to indicate the entrance to Ostrich Creek through which a small stream, Belstead Brook enters the river after passing under Bourne Bridge. The last buoy with a light is the red can Factory buoy (QR) off the container terminal, although there are several more unlit buoys leading right up to the entrance to the Wet Dock.

Ostrich Creek

The Orwell YC has both drying and deep water moorings on the W side of the river up to the West Bank Container Dock. There is a visitor's mooring near No 12 channel buoy and a floating pontoon accessible at all times.

There is a small pool just to the E of the pontoon, with three posts to which visitors may moor overnight – given permission from the Orwell YC.

For day to day requirements, it is not really necessary to go farther afield than the vicinity of the clubhouse and Bourne Bridge. The Oyster Reach Beefeater pub, formerly The Ostrich inn, is nearby.

An aerial view of the Orwell, showing Fox's Marina and Ostrich Creek at the bottom left of the picture, and the Wet Dock with Neptune Marina in the heart of Ipswich at the top right

Neptune Marina is situated on the Historic Waterfront in Ipswich's famous Wet Dock, with very good access to the centre of Suffolk's county town

Port Guide: Bourne Bridge

Fox's Marina Tel:	(01473) 689111 VHF Ch 80 and 37 M
Orwell Yacht Club	Tel: (01473) 602288
Water	From clubhouse or marina pontoons
Stores	Shops nearby
Petrol and Oil	Garage adjacent to clubhouse
Gas	From marina
Chandlery	At marina, open 7 days a week
Repairs	Travelifts and extensive facilities at marina boatyard
Transport	Buses into Ipswich (1½ miles). Good train service from Ipswich to London
Telephone	From club or box nearby and at marina
Clubs	Orwell Yacht Club. Fox's Marina YC

Fox's Marina

This 100-berth marina and boatyard is situated next to Bourne Bridge (abreast No 12 buoy). Entrance is through a dredged gutway marked on both sides by beacons. Facilities include travel lifts, workshops and a very large chandlery.

Ipswich Dock

When it was opened in 1850 the Wet Dock at Ipswich was the largest in Europe and right up to the 1930s it was being used by square rigged grain ships. The 100-berth Neptune Marina is in the Dock at Neptune Quay, on the Historic Waterfront, to the east of the Old Custom House. Yard facilities include a 40 ton travel hoist; shops and restaurants are nearby, and Ipswich town centre is within a 10 minute walk.

When planning to enter the Dock a yacht should contact Ipswich Port radio when at No 9 buoy, to check the time of opening the lock gates. Then contact Neptune Marina for berthing arrangements. There is a pontoon against which a boat can lie outside the lock while awaiting its opening.

The Dock is approached along a closely buoyed channel past the Ro-Ro terminal opposite Cliff Quay. The lock gates and swing bridge open from about 2 hours before HW until 40 minutes after that. Red and green traffic control lights are located above the Orwell Navigation Service building on the E side of the lock.

Yachts should not berth alongside any of the commercial quays without first obtaining permission from the Port Authority.

New Cut

Above the lock and to port is New Cut with Debbage's yard just upstream providing drying pontoon moorings, water and diesel fuel, repairs and a 20-ton crane; shops nearby (EC Wed). Ipswich station is about half a mile away. There is a water velocity control structure within the entrance to New Cut: when 3 vertical red lights show, the structure is raised and vessels may not proceed.

Port Guide: Ipswich

Harbourmaster	Tel: (01473) 211771
Ipswich Port Radio	VHF Ch 14
Neptune Marina	Tel:(01473) 215204 (dockside) 780366 (office) VHF Ch 14 (at tide times)
Debbage's Yard	Tel: (01473) 601169
Stores	Nearby and at town centre.
Restaurants	On quayside and nearby
Water	Neptune Marina pontoons
Fuel	Diesel and petrol (own cans) near Marina. Gas at Marina
Repairs	Travel lift, cranes, shipwrights, engineering, rigging and full yard facilities at Marina
Transport	Good train service Ipswich-London
Telephone	Near Marina

7. The River Stour

Tides (Wrabness): HW Dover +01.05 Range: Springs 3.7m Neaps 2.3m
Charts: Admiralty 2693, Stanford No 6, Imray Y16
Waypoints: Guard Buoy 51.57.07N 01.17.88E. Stour No 12 Buoy 51.56.92N 01.06.10E
Hazards: Ferries turning off Parkeston Quay

The river Stour has never been as popular with yachtsmen as the Orwell and this is probably due to a number of reasons; Parkeston Quay with its attendant movements of large ferries, the absence of any waterside hamlet to compare with Pin Mill and the difficulty of lying afloat out of the fairway anywhere above Wrabness.

Yet the Stour is quieter and more spacious than the Orwell and, moreover, its twin towns – Mistley and Manningtree – have been called 'two of the best-looking places in Essex.'

Frequent ferries and a high speed Sea Cat operate from the Ro Ro terminals at Parkeston Quay, but it is not diffficult to keep clear of them, since even at low water the channel is almost half a mile wide. However, it is true that beyond Wrabness the width of the low-tide channel narrows rather abruptly. Although well buoyed, it does involve a risk of grounding, particularly when a first passage is attempted while the wide mud flats are covered. But this objection is not peculiar to the Stour, since much the same conditions are found in the upper tidal reaches of almost all the rivers of the Thames Estuary.

Channel Widths

The navigable channel extends from Harwich to Manningtree, some nine miles. The Stour separates the counties of Essex and Suffolk, and its general direction is westerly throughout the eight miles or so to Mistley. At high tide the river appears to be a mile or more wide throughout the whole of its length. In fact its width at LW, while nearly half a mile abreast Shotley Pier and much the same from there to Harkstead Point, diminishes rapidly thereafter to about two cables off Wrabness Point and up as far as Stutton Ness. Then, along the mile or so of Straight Reach, the channel again narrows to less than a cable just below Ballast Hill. The final reaches between Ballast Hill and Mistley Quay become narrower still, until abreast the quays the channel at LW is less than 50 metres wide.

The most useful anchorage in the entrance to the Stour is over on the north bank of the river close to Shotley Pier. Anchorage is prohibited in the vicinity of Parkston Quay. The first useful small boat anchorage above Harwich Harbour is off Erwarton Ness, about a mile and a half W of Parkeston.

There are two starboard hand marks between Parkeston

The Stena Line runs a high speed sea cat ferry twice daily from Harwich to The Hook – this aerial view is of the terminal at Parkeston on the River Stour

Quay and Harkstead Point; first a S. Cardinal beacon (Q (6)+ LF1(2)15s) and then a green conical buoy (QG). The depth of the water in the channel is never less than 5m, until about a mile below Harkstead Point, when the mid-river water shallows gradually from about 5m to 3.5m abreast the Point.

Erwarton Ness

With any north in the wind there is a good anchorage off Erwarton Ness about a cable from the derelict quay in line with the S cardinal beacon (Q F1(6) LF1 15s). There is good holding in mud, but no protection from either easterly or westerly winds. Landing is possible near the ruined staithe between half-flood and half-ebb. Erwarton village is about a mile away, although the inn, the Queen's Head, is a little nearer.

Holbrook Bay

Continuing up-river from Erwarton Ness, Harkstead Point is the next low headland on the north shore, while on the south bank, Wrabness Point is notable for its height (40ft) in East Coast waters. Once clear of Harkstead Point and the S cardinal

Holbrook beacon (Q Fl(6) LFl 15s), the scene to the north will open out to disclose the extensive buildings and conspicuous central spire of the Royal Hospital School on the high ground at Holbrook. When the tide has no more than half flooded, the extensive mud flats of Holbrook Bay cover an area roughly two miles long and a mile deep. Two or three ill-defined creeks lead across these flats, the more important of them being Gallister Creek and Holbrook Creek.

Gallister Creek

There is enough water and just enough space to lie quietly to an anchor a cable or so inside Gallister Creek, but for landing it is probably better to use Holbrook Creek.

Holbrook Creek

This creek is marked by withies along its western edge and there is enough depth and space to allow anchoring for a quarter of a mile inside. Any exploring farther up the creek should be done just before the mud banks are covered and while the gutway can be followed.

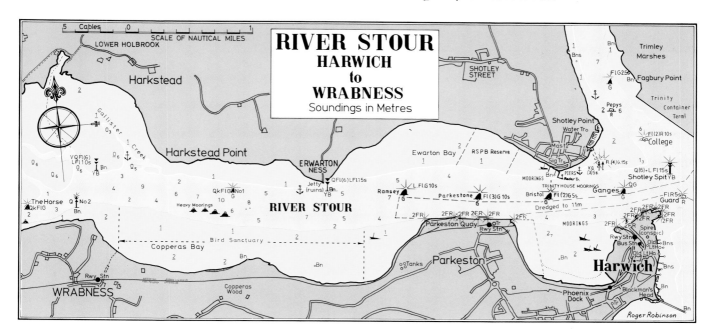

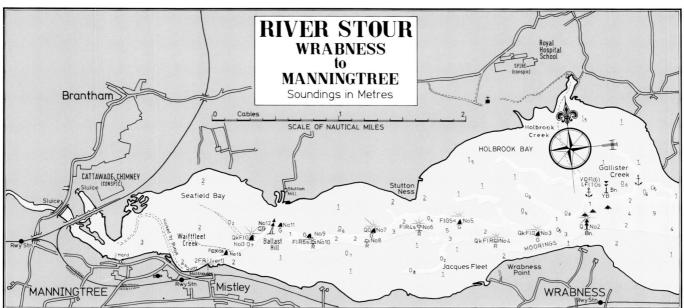

Holbrook Creek is shallow and winding, but can be entered by light draught boats or dinghies. There is clean landing at the head of the creek and a lane leading to the village of Harkstead

Clean landing is possible at the head of Holbrook Creek near HW, and Holbrook village and stores are about a mile away.

Wrabness Point

There used to be a horse in mid-stream off Wrabness, but following extensive dredging for shingle this now seems to have merged with the flats on Holbrook Bay so that the only channel now runs close to the point, past a port hand N cardinal beacon (Q) and a conical green (QG) starboard hand buoy. Because of previous dredging for shingle, the holding ground in the channel off Wrabness is not as safe as it used to be and if there is no vacant mooring, it will usually pay to move a bit further upstream towards the next port hand buoy. In any case beware of anchoring in mid-channel because of the commercial shipping using Mistley Quay. If stopping overnight, a riding light is essential.

There is no yard or club at Wrabness, so it would be unwise to leave a boat on a vacant mooring.

The village of Wrabness is reached by climbing a pathway up the cliff and following the lane past the church towards the railway station. The church is one of the two in this district which have their bells in a wooden cage-like belfry in the churchyard.

A television mast on the south side of the river provides a conspicuous mark by day and by night.

When continuing up-river from Wrabness a stranger to the Stour will do well to set off before the mud flats are covered and while the course of the channel is visible as well as the buoys which mark it. In these narrow upper reaches the buoys must be given a wide berth whenever it appears that they are being swept by the tide over the banks they are intended to mark.

From the anchorage off Wrabness the channel turns a little N of W for about a mile, past a port hand buoy (QR) and a conical green buoy (Fl G 5s) to starboard. Jacques Fleet and the bay of the same name are to the south; a few barges may sometimes be lying here.

The next mark is No 6 Beacon (Fl R 4s) with a tide gauge, marking Smith Shoal; it is located about three cables south of Stutton Ness, and the best water here is no more than two cables from the Suffolk shore.

West of Stutton Ness the channel continues for a mile along Straight Reach, becoming narrower and shallower. There are three conical green buoys to be left to starboard and three red cans to be left to port along this reach. Then comes a bottleneck at Ballast Hill, where for a short distance there is a depth of only 1m and a width of less than a cable at LW. The port hand at Ballast Hill is the N cardinal No 12 (QR).

Use of the sounder or sounding pole offers the best chance of getting through here early on the tide. Once past the shingle patch that forms Ballast Hill, there is an isolated widening and deepening of the channel in Cross Reach. This hole provides the only spot in which a boat drawing 1.5m of water can remain afloat within reasonable distance of Mistley.

After Cross Reach the channel turns south-westerly along Waiftfleet Reach and Miller Reach and from hereabouts the warehouses and maltings and the twin towers of the ruined Adam church at Mistley will all come into view.

Port Guide: Wrabness	
Water	From standpipe at top of cliff
Stores	Obtainable in village. EC Wed
Transport	Train service to London

The buoyage and marking of the winding channel of the river between Wrabness and Mistley Quay have been changed considerably several times in the last few years and this has made it very difficult to provide information that will remain reliable throughout the life of an edition.

Westwards from Baltic Wharf the best water will be found within twenty or thirty metres of the quayside. The depths here at LW are nowhere more than about 1m and one of the few holes having this much water should be sought opposite a small dock or basin about half-way along the quays.

There is good holding in the channel at Mistley, but the tide runs very hard during the first half of the ebb, when the rate can be as high as 4 knots. At Mistley it is HW 50 minutes later than at Harwich.

Landing at the quayside by means of one of the several vertical ladders is not very easy, except at high water, but it is worthwhile going ashore at Mistley to walk to the top of Furze Hill and enjoy the fine view of the river from there and to see the famous twin towers that remain from the church that Robert Adam designed in 1776.

Above Mistley

Manningtree can be reached in craft drawing as much as 2m, provided the buoys are carefully observed, and the ship is prepared to take the ground soon after arrival at Manningtree. In a shallower draught boat, drawing no more than 1m, it is also possible, just before HW, to take the North or Second channel across Seafield Bay direct from Ballast Hill to the bend

Facilities at Manningtree	
Water	From quayside
Stores	Shops in town. EC Wed
Petrol and oil	Garages nearby
Transport	Direct train service to London
Club	Stour Sailing Club

in the channel known as the Hook. But if you are sailing across the flats off Mistley, look out for the wreck that lies there.

The local centreboard classes belonging to the members of the Stour Sailing Club race around a course which takes them right across Seafield Bay to within a cable or so of the Suffolk shore.

The quay at Manningtree is not so extensive as at Mistley, and there is no water at all at low tide.

It is only a ten or 15 minute walk to Manningtree from Mistley along a pleasant riverside road.

Port Guide: Mistley	
Water	From the quay
Stores	Several shops in main street near quay. EC Wed
Petrol and oil	From garage
Transport	Train service to London

A turn in the course of the river Stour takes it alongside the interesting town of Mistley, once famous for its spritsail barges

8. The Walton Backwaters

Tides (Stone Point): HW Dover + 0040 Range: Springs 3.6m Neaps 2.1m
Charts: Admiralty 2692, Stanford No 6, Imray Y16
Waypoints: Stone Banks Buoy 51.53.16N 01.19.33E. Pye-End Buoy 51.55.00N 01.18.00E
Hazards: Lines of lobster pots off Walton-on-the-Naze

The map that Arthur Ransome's Swallows and Amazons drew of their 'secret waters' would still serve quite well for navigating the Walton Backwaters, for little has changed, except the number of boats. All the creeks give good protection in almost any weather, and the Backwaters are an excellent base from which to make a number of modest cruises to the Stour, the Orwell or the Deben.

Approaches

The entrance to the Backwaters is located about half a mile off the Dovercourt foreshore, and half a mile or so south of the mouth of Harwich Harbour. Whether approaching from the north or the south, it is necessary to find Pye-End buoy, (Sph.RW L Fl 10s) marking the northern extremity of an area of hard sand known as Pye Sand and the Sunken Pye.

When approaching Harwich from the south through the Wallet and the Medusa channel the most prominent landmark is the Naze Tower, erected by Trinity House in 1720, and standing 160ft above the cliffs just north of Walton-on-the-Naze.

Another conspicuous landmark was added in 1992 in the

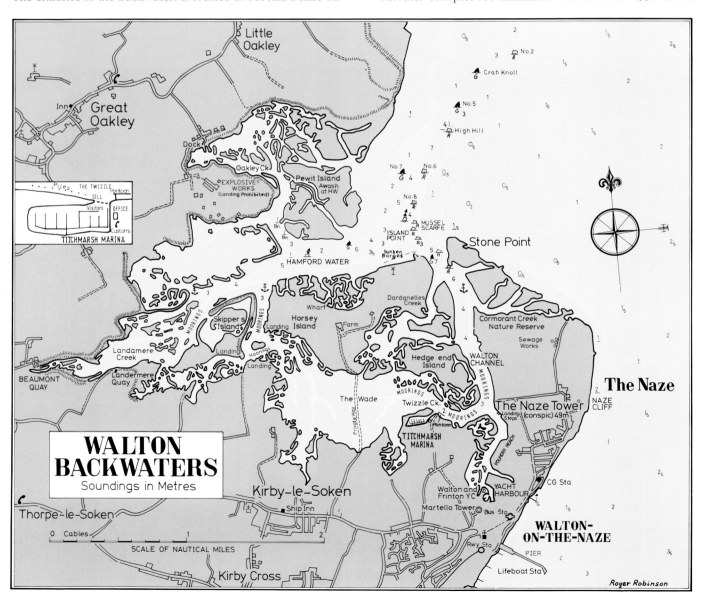

WALTON BACKWATERS
Soundings in Metres

form of the 57m radar mast located on the cliff-top between Frinton and Clacton.

The Medusa buoy (Con G Fl G 5s) lies just over two miles E of Walton pier and, from a position midway between the pier and the Medusa, the Naze Tower will bear approximately NW while the next mark, the Stone Banks buoy (Can R can topmark), will lie about three miles away to the NNE. Any less than a mile offshore around the Naze will probably have you bumping the bottom. There is considerable erosion of the cliffs, and as a result a shoal patch seems to be spreading out beneath the tower.

Another problem hereabouts is the multitude of lobster pots that are set by inshore fishermen. However hard one tries it is difficult to avoid them in poor visibility and practically impossible at night. So, if you find your progress seems slower than usual, see whether you have a line and pot caught by your rudder or prop.

In good visibility such landmarks as the tall spire of St Nicholas Church at Harwich and the large cranes at the Port of Felixstowe will be seen before the Stone Banks buoy comes up. This buoy, as its name suggests, marks a number of isolated clumps of stones and rocks with no more than 2m over them at LWS. A course only slightly W of N from the Stone Banks buoy will bring Harwich breakwater (awash at HW) in view ahead. When about a mile from the breakwater and the entrance to Harwich Harbour it should be possible in conditions of reasonable visibility to spot the Pye-End buoy (Sph RW LFl 10s) which is located approximately 1 mile due S (mag) from the end of the breakwater and is now the responsibility of the Harwich Harbour Board.

The buildings along the shore of Dovercourt Bay provide a background which makes it rather difficult to locate the buoy.

The shallowest part of the approach to the Backwaters is the area known as the Halliday Rock Flats where there is less than 2m in places during LWS. This shoal water will prevent many craft from attempting the entrance before two or three hours of flood. It is HWFC hereabouts at approximately midday and midnight. Springs rise 4m and neaps 3m.

When approaching the Backwaters from the north, the well-buoyed big-ship channel should be crossed as quickly as possible and then followed, outside it, as far as the Landguard buoy (N Card YB Q) from which a course of approximately 245°M will lead to the Pye-End Buoy less than a mile away. This same course, if continued, should find the No 2 red can buoy at the entrance to the channel into the Backwaters.

The narrow channel into the Walton Backwaters over the Pye Sands has been marked for the past 75 years by buoys supplied and maintained by the Walton and Frinton Yacht Club, and in order to ease the cost of laying and raising them the Club has arranged for local firms to sponsor some of them. In 1995 the club established a light on the existing High Hill buoy to assist local craft using the channel at night.

However, even in bright daylight, the newcomer will look to the SW from abreast the Pye-End buoy and find it difficult to believe that any kind of deep water channel lies ahead. But after sailing in a generally south-westerly direction for a quarter of a mile or so, the next buoys – No 2, a red can buoy, and No 3 (Crab Knoll), a green buoy with iron strapping to form a conical top, will come into view. The Dovercourt shore shelves regularly, and is the safer side to work until this first

The Pye End buoy needs to be located when approaching the entrance to Walton Backwaters

pair of buoys have been reached, after which the channel becomes narrower and deeper, and the sand is steep-to on either hand.

The next green conical buoy, No 5, is about half a mile further to the SW, and it marks the western edge of the channel where it narrows to a bottleneck, little more than a cable wide, at a point known as High Hill, marked by a lit red can buoy bearing that name (Fl R 10 radar reflector). There are eight or nine metres of water in the channel here, but since the sand on either side is quite steep-to, short boards are essential whenever it is necessary to turn to windward, and continuous use of the echo sounder, or very smart use of the lead, is the only sure guide to the limits of the channel, when the tide has covered the banks and there are no ripples. It is also as well to remember that spring tides run out of here at 2½ knots during the first part of the ebb. From High Hill onwards, the channel widens to two or three cables and is marked on the W side by a green conical buoy (No 7) and on the E side by red cans (Nos 6 and 8). From hereabouts it is usually possible to see the Horsey Island Point buoy (N Card) at the junction of Hamford Water and the Walton Channel.

Entrance to Walton Channel

When bound for the Walton Channel there are three more unnumbered red can buoys to be left to port round Mussel Scarfe. This series of buoys should not be passed too closely because under certain conditions of tide and westerly wind they can be over the bank they mark. Neither should the Island Point buoy be approached too closely when entering or leaving the Walton Channel, as there is an extension of the mud bank to the E, just south of the buoy. A green conical buoy marks this hazard.

The last two port-hand buoys mark the NW and W edge of Stone Point respectively. The outer (northernmost) of these two also indicates the SW end of a channel known as 'The Swatch', which is used (near HW), by local craft bound for the fishing grounds off the Naze.

During the summer months the warden is often on duty in Walton Backwaters, in the launch Gamebird

Stone Point

The steep-to shingle bank at Stone Point provides a popular landing place at all states of the tide, while the anchorage nearby offers excellent protection. The holding ground in the channel is good, but the depths are considerable and, since the ebb runs hard in midstream, as much as 3 knots during springs, it is preferable to anchor close to the E bank, where there is a slight contra-flow eddy during the first part of the ebb.

On a fine day in summer, Walton Stone Point is a good spot for a bathe and picnic, but it is a privately owned bird sanctuary and nature reserve. Unfortunately some unthinking people light fires, leave rubbish and trample down the plants and grass that are so important to the wild life of the area. If this kind of thoughtless behaviour were to continue Stone Point might be prohibited to yachtsmen but fortunately the Point is under the control of the Walton and Frinton Yacht Club, whom we must certainly support.

The Walton Channel is not buoyed between Stone Point and the Twizzle, but the best water is to be found midway between the banks, except near the mouth of Stone Creek, where mud extends to the W, and the channel is nearer the Horsey Island shore. The depths in the channel decrease from 7m off Stone Point to rather less than 5m where the creek changes direction and name and becomes the Twizzle, at the entrance to which there is a shoal area.

There are many moorings in the Walton Channel below the junction with Foundry Reach, but even more craft are moored in the Twizzle, which carries a depth of nearly two metres for about a mile. Some very small craft are permanently moored in Foundry Reach, but as this dries out for most of its length it is only of use to larger craft towards HW when, on a good tide, they can berth alongside the clubhouse of the Walton and Frinton YC long enough to take on water or even to do some shopping in the town.

The landing at the clubhouse can be reached by dinghy for all but an hour on either side of LW. Visitors to the Backwaters are always welcome at the club.

If the tide does not suit, or the long trip to the clubhouse from the Twizzle is unattractive, it is possible to land from a dinghy at some concrete steps built on to the sea wall of the E bank of Foundry Creek, just above its junction with the Twizzle. From these steps or a nearby slip, it is a walk of about a mile into Walton, and even longer to the clubhouse, but by taking a footpath nearby, general stores and a telephone box near the Naze can be reached more easily than those at Walton.

The Walton-on-the-Naze Yacht Basin is adjacent to the Walton and Frinton Yacht Club in Mill Lane. This yacht basin has retaining gates that are opened around the time of high water (approximately 20 min after HW Harwich) when there is a depth of about 2m in the entrance at neap tides and about 2.5m at springs. (It is not always possible to open the gates on some neap tides and in any case they are opened only during working hours.)

Port Guide: Walton-on-the-Naze	
Water	From alongside the clubhouse
Stores	Shops ¼ mile from clubhouse. EC Wed
Petrol and oil	From garages in town. Diesel from yard near quay
Repairs	Several shipwrights in Mill Lane, near club. Derrick available. Sailmaker in Town
Transport	Trains to London via Colchester. Buses to Colchester, Clacton and Harwich
Walton Yacht Basin	Tel: (01255) 675873
Club	Walton and Frinton Yacht Club
Telephone	At clubhouse

Entering Hamford Water on the top of the tide

The Twizzle

The Twizzle, which runs in a generally westerly direction, is really a continuation of Walton Channel, and it offers complete protection in an average depth of 2m at LW except near its entrance. Craft are moored on both sides of the Twizzle and anchoring is certainly not advisable because many of the ground chains are laid across the channel. After enquiry at the clubhouse or one of the local yards it is sometimes possible to borrow one of the moorings for a short period. Those marked with a 'B' belong to Bedwells, while those with an 'H' are owned by Halls.

There is clean landing on shingle at Colonel's Hard about two cables inside the Twizzle, on the S shore of the creek. The Walton Lifeboat is sometimes moored off this hard, from which the town can be reached by walking along the sea wall.

Titchmarsh Marina

The Titchmarsh Marina (450 boats) is on the S side of the Twizzle, a little to the W of Colonel's Hard. There is about 2m of water in the basin, but very little over the sill in the entrance at LW neaps and this means, as it does at several other east coast marinas, that no boats can leave or enter at LW springs. But in this case there is a line of dolphins and a pontoon in the Twizzle nearby and, as they belong to the marina, boats can lie there while they wait for water over the sill.

The marina is a fair way from the town of Walton-on-the-Naze, so you may need to use the telephone box to call a taxi. There is no longer a Customs Post at the marina, but the Customs boat, Lynx, is based there.

The Twizzle is navigable at LW by craft drawing 1m as far as the western end of Hedge End Island – about a mile from the entrance of Foundry Creek. Farther W, the Twizzle becomes a narrow, winding gutway through the extensive mud and saltings of Horsey Mere. The gutway is marked by a confusion of withies that would require much acquaintance to

Port Guide: Titchmarsh Marina	
Harbourmaster	Tel: (01255) 851899
	VHF Channels M 37 and 80
Water	On pontoons
Stores	Small selection at chandlery. Local delivery service from Walton
Diesel	On site
Gas	From chandlery
Repairs	35 ton travel-lift, marine engineers
Restaurant and bar	On site

understand. The creek finally peters out to the E of the rough roadway known as the Wade, which crosses Horsey Mere to join the mainland with the farm on Horsey Island.

There are oyster beds at the extreme W end of the Twizzle, so care must be taken not to ground in this area.

Those who have read Arthur Ransome's Secret Water will remember the exciting race the 'Explorers' had when they crossed the Wade during a rising tide.

It is possible to sail straight across Horsey Mere from the Twizzle to Kirby Creek, provided the boat does not draw more than about 1m and the trip is made about an hour before HW, on a day near to, but before, spring tides.

Hamford Water

Hamford Water is also known as the West Water. It runs in a generally south-westerly direction from the Island Point buoy moored off the mud spit extending from the north-eastern corner of Horsey Island, to the north-eastern end of Skipper's Island, where the channel divides. There is plenty of water in this main reach of Hamford Water – 7m near the entrance, and 5m about a mile inside. The width of the channel is nearly two cables at LW and the N side of it is marked by a green coni-

This view of Titchmarsh Marina looking to the north, shows Hamford Water and Oakley Creek beyond

cal buoy. Both protection and holding are excellent, unless you are unlucky enough to drop your hook on top of one of the massive growths of 'pipe weed' that have infested these waters in recent years. When any kind of anchor lands on a patch of this stuff its holding power becomes negligible. It is therefore a good idea to test (under power if necessary) that your anchor is holding before settling down for the night and certainly before leaving the boat.

Oakley Creek

Oakley Creek branches to the north, out of Hamford Water and between Bramble and Pewit Islands. The spit off the W side of the entrance is marked by a N cardinal buoy. There is enough water for light draught craft to lie afloat for nearly a mile within, but it is probably best to resist any temptation to anchor there because the creek is used once or twice a week by freighters which load at the wharf belonging to an explosives factory at Oakley, where landing is s trictly prohibited.

Landermere Creek

By continuing west along Hamford Water, a boat drawing up to 2m can safely reach the division of the channel where Landermere Creek turns towards Landermere Quay. There are some moorings just beyond here but usually enough space and depth to anchor clear of them. Landing from a dinghy is possible at the quay from about half-flood. Stores must be sought at Thorpe-le-Soken.

At around high water it is possible to take a dinghy beyond Landermere up to Beaumont Quay, where a plaque will inform you that the stones used for its construction came from the old London Bridge. An overhead power cable spans the cut and prevents boats with masts from reaching the quay. The quay is only a quarter of a mile from a main-road bus route to Thorpe-le-Soken, where there are shops from which most stores can be obtained.

Kirby Creek

This creek joins Hamford Water on its S side about a quarter mile beyond Oakley Creek, offering one of the most popular anchorages in the Backwaters.

The Naze Oyster Company has some of its layings in Kirby Creek and, like anywhere else that oysters are cultivated, a yachtsman is responsible if by anchoring or grounding he damages any of the stock. Notice boards to this effect will be seen at the entrance to the creek.

If for some reason conditions in Hamford Water are uncomfortable, yachtsmen may be able to anchor just within Kirby Creek and above the layings, but then they must beware the treacherously long spit of mud that extends from the NE end of Skipper's Island.

Skipper's Island is used by the Essex Naturalists' Society, and they have erected an observation tower from which they can watch the many species of birds that come to the Backwaters. For stores a landing can be made at a wooden staithe on the mainland opposite the SE corner of the Island. This is a good landing except at dead low water, but the walk along the sea wall to Kirby-le-Soken is about a mile and a half.

From abreast the wooden staithe Kirby Creek turns sharply to the E, to emerge into Horsey Mere, and then turns S again up to Kirby Quay. The quay can be reached by dinghy towards HW, and the tortuous gutway is plentifully marked by withies, which are no doubt understood by local sailors, but at first acquaintance are only likely to baffle the uninitiated.

The village of Kirby-le-Soken is no more than a quarter of a mile from the quay, and the village shops will satisfy a yachtsman's day-to-day needs.

9. The River Colne

Tides (Brightlingsea): HW Dover + 0.55 Range: Springs 4.6m Neaps 2.6m (HW Colchester approx 20 mins after HW Brightlingsea)
Charts: Admiralty 3741, Stanford No 4, Imray Y170
Waypoints: Knoll Buoy 51.43.85N 01.05.17E. NW Knoll Buoy 51.44.32N 01.02.27E. Inner Bench Head Buoy 51.45.93N 01.01.86E.
Hazards: Knoll, Colne Bar and Bench Head shoals near LW

Not since the days of the trading barges has the riverColne been so busy with commercial traffic as it is again now. Small freighters berth regularly at Colchester or Wivenhoe and some also call at Brightlingsea.

But for many people the Colne is known for its oysters – still cultivated in Pyefleet Creek, as they were when the Romans were at Colchester. Every October the Mayor, accompanied by officials of the Colchester Oyster Company, celebrate the start of a new season while moored in Pyefleet Creek.

The river Colne is smaller and more intimate that its close neighbour, the Blackwater. Both these rivers join the sea at the NW Knoll buoy, midway between Colne Point to the E and Sales Point to the W. The distance from the Knoll buoy to the Hythe at Colchester is about 11 miles, most of which lies in a north-north-westerly direction.

Approaches from Seaward

When approaching the Colne from the S through the Swin Spitway or from the N, up the Wallet, make for the Knoll buoy (N Car Q) and then leave both the Eagle (Con G QG) and the Colne Bar (Con G Fl(2)G 5s) buoys close to starboard before shaping a course of 350°M into the entrance of the river. From a position near the Bar buoy a group of three more buoys will usually be seen in daylight – the Fishery buoy (Spher Y), the Colne Point buoy (Con G) and the Inner Bench Head (Can R Fl(2)R 5s).

Shoal draught boats can, provided it is not too near the time of low water, cross Colne Bar north of the Eagle and as much as a mile inside the Bar buoy. When coming south a sudden increase in depths will indicate when the bar has been crossed.

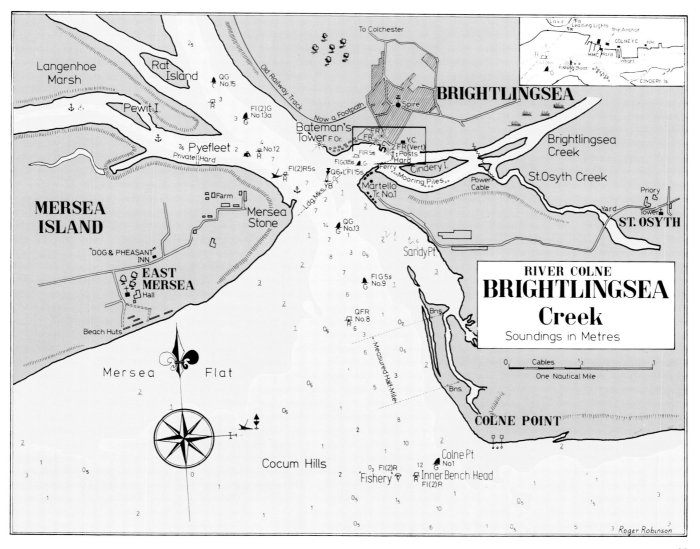

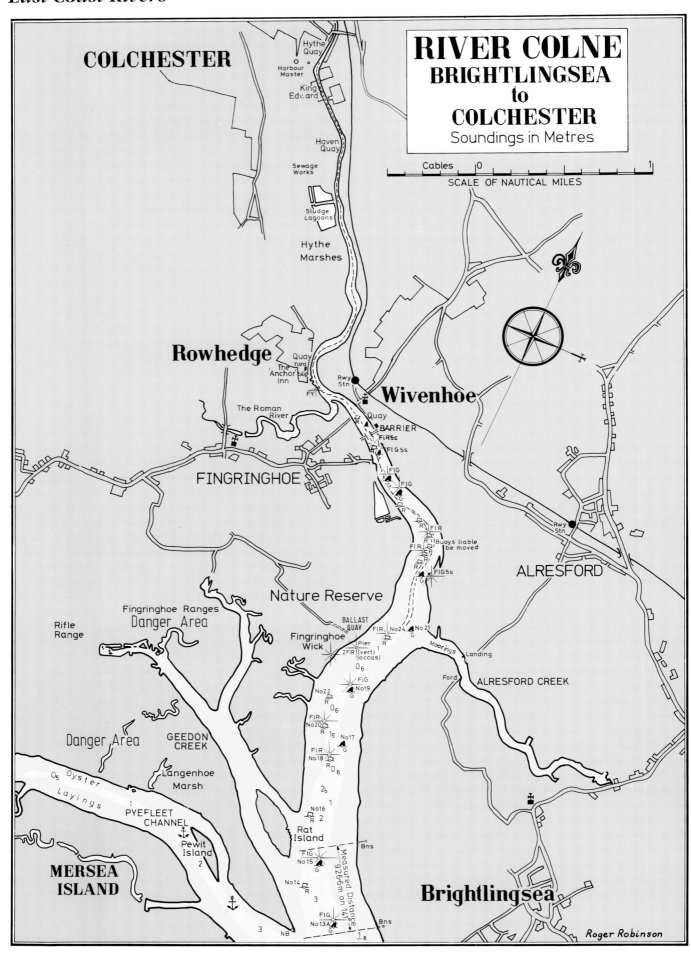

COLCHESTER

Hythe Quay

Harbour Master

King Edward

Haven Quay

Sewage Works

Sludge Lagoons

Hythe Marshes

RIVER COLNE
BRIGHTLINGSEA
to
COLCHESTER
Soundings in Metres

Cables   0   1
SCALE OF NAUTICAL MILES

Rowhedge

Quay Yard
The Anchor Inn
FY

The Roman River

Rwy Stn

Wivenhoe

Quay
BARRIER
FlR5s
FlG5s

FINGRINGHOE

FlG

G   FlG

R

R   FlR
R   Buoys liable
       be moved
FlR   R
R
G   FlG5s

ALRESFORD

Rwy Stn

Nature Reserve

Fingringhoe Ranges
Danger Area

Rifle Range

BALLAST QUAY

FlR   No24   No21
G   G

Moorings   Landing

Ford   **ALRESFORD CREEK**

Fingringhoe Wick
2FR (vert) (occas)   Pier 1
0.6

No22   FlG
R   No19
0.6   G

FlR
No20   1.5   No17
R   G

Danger Area   GEEDON CREEK

Langenhoe Marsh

FlR
No18   0.6
R

2.5
1

No16   2
R

Rat Island

Oyster Layings
0.5
1
PYEFLEET CHANNEL

Pewit Island
2

MERSEA ISLAND

Bns

FlG
No15
G

No14
R   3

3

FlG
No13A
G

Measured Distance
9266m on 14°

Bns

1.8

Brightlingsea

NB   3

Roger Robinson

Pontoon and pile moorings at Brightlingsea in the creek running south of Cindery Island

From the Inner Bench Head light buoy inwards, the channel is buoyed on both sides – even numbered red cans to port and odd-numbered green conical buoys to starboard. There is a depth of some 9m between the first pair of channel buoys, and there is not much less than 6m anywhere within the channel until abreast the entrance to Brightlingsea Creek. However, carefully observe the buoys on both hands, since the water shoals quite rapidly, particularly to the W.

When sailing to the Blackwater from the Colne it is safe, except near low water, for craft drawing 2m or less to cross from the deep water of the Colne on a course that has St Peters Chapel (near Sales Point) bearing 240 degrees M. This will lead about midway between the Bench Head and Cocum Hills shoals.

In clear weather, from a position abreast the Inner Bench Head it is possible to see Brightlingsea Church tower on high ground, due N (mag), distant four miles. Another mark that will help the newcomer get his bearings is the very large building shed at Brightlingsea, which may be seen over the low-lying shore from several miles away.

Brightlingsea Creek

The buoy at the entrance to Brightlingsea Creek is a South Cardinal yellow and black buoy (QFl(6)LFl 15s). The entrance it marks is very shallow, with not much more than 1m best water at LWS. A conical green buoy (Fl(3)G 5s) inside the entrance is intended to keep you off the spit that extends from St Osyth Stone Point, while a red can (FlR 5s) marks the northern edge of the channel.

The correct course into the creek itself is 42°M and by day this line is indicated by two leading marks (orange and white stripes) known locally as the 'cricket stumps' and set up on poles in the town. By night these marks bear two fixed red leading lights.

Port Guide: Brightlingsea

Harbourmaster	Tel (01206) 302200 VHF Ch 68
Hard master	Tel (01206) 303535
Water Taxi	VHF Ch 37
Water	Tap at top of hard; or CYC pontoon by arrangement
Stores	Shops in town (½ mile). EC Thurs
Chandler	Near town hard
Petrol and oil	From chandlers
Repairs	Yards nearby
Sailmaker	In Tower Street
Transport	Buses to Colchester, whence good train service to London
Clubs	Colne Yacht Club (tel: 01206 302594). Brightlingsea Sailing Club
Telephone	At top of hard

Batemans Tower, although condemned at one time, is now safe and lit with an orange sodium lamp.

Most of the local yachts at Brightlingsea are moored fore and aft, rafted together (3 boats in each bay) between two lines of piles in the creek running S of Cindery Island. At low water there is only about 1.5m and even less on the E side of the posts.

The first few piles in the northern row have been replaced by pontoons where some local boats have permanent berths. However, visitors can often be accommodated after checking with the harbour master, who can usually be found in his dinghy around high water. From April to September there is a regular and inexpensive water taxi service to the shore.

There is little water in the creek that runs to the N of Cindery Island, and on up to the head of the creek, where there is a jetty used by gravel barges. Because of this traffic, which can be at night, there are no moorings to the N of Cindery Island and a fairway must be maintained at all times.

Brightlingsea offers excellent facilities to the yachtsman. There is a fine hard on which almost any boat can stand upright against one of the several posts available. Arrangements for using the posts should be made with the Hard Master whose office is near the YC jetty; he is in attendance from Monday to Friday in the mornings only.

The Colne YC has a catwalk and pontoon by the clubhouse just E of the town causeway; visitors are welcome, meals and showers can usually be obtained.

St Osyth Creek

Above Brightlingsea, there are two tidal islands – W and E Cindery Islands, dividing Brightlingsea Creek into two branches, abreast the junction with St Osyth Creek. This latter creek is no more than a mile long and is very narrow, particularly near the entrance where the best water (perhaps as much as 1.5m at LW) will be found between a tiny hummock of land known as Pincushion Island and the S bank. Shallow draught boats can safely reach the head of the creek for about an hour or so either side of HW. The creek is sparsely marked by withies.

St Osyth itself is worth visiting to see the remains of the twelfth century Priory, although all signs of the tide-mill have now disappeared. There is a boatyard with a crane and slip and a chandler near the quay, which is wooden faced and has several ladders. This is a popular venue for owners of Essex smacks.

East Mersea Point

Opposite the entrance to Brightlingsea Creek is Mersea Point – the eastern extremity of Mersea Island. There is a good landing on the shingle of Mersea Point, and one can walk to the Dog and Pheasant, about a mile away.

Good holding ground in 5m, well protected from all but south or south-easterly winds, can be found clear of the few moorings and between Mersea Point and the old wreck that dries out just below the entrance to Pyefleet Creek. This wreck, of a ship called Lowlands, is marked by a red can buoy (Fl(2)R 5s).

Since chartered sailing barges and coasters frequently bring up off the entrance to Brightlingsea Creek, it is essential to use a riding light when anchored at night.

Pyefleet Creek

A cable or two above the wreck on the W side of the river is the entrance to Pyfleet Creek – an important oyster preserve – which nevertheless provides an excellent anchorage with good protection. In fact, an anchorage in Pyefleet is usually more comfortable than a berth within Brightlingsea Creek, because of the swell that often enters the creek at the turn of the tide.

Pyefleet Creek is one of the most popular Saturday night anchorages on the whole of the East Coast. Perhaps this is because it provides that sense of remoteness for which so many of us feel a need. There are no landing places and no cars in sight and although there may be twenty or thirty craft at anchor, everyone (except the waterskiers) is there for the peace and quiet and acts accordingly.

The deep water in the entrance to Pyefleet is indicated by a line of mooring buoys, belonging to the Colchester Oyster Company, who may charge for their use. There is plenty of room and plenty of water for a mile or more up the creek, and yachts may bring up either just within the entrance or anywhere up to or even above Pewit Island, which is easily recognised by its oyster packing sheds. Great care must be taken to avoid anchoring or grounding on any of the oyster layings in the Pyefleet. Craft drawing up to 2m can remain afloat as far us as Maydays Marsh, where the channel divides; the S branch leading to the Strood which joins Mersea Island to the mainland.

The only disadvantage of the Pyefleet anchorage is that no supplies are available nearer than Brightlingsea, which can seem a long way when a strong wind is blowing up or down the Colne. At weekends during the summer it is possible to buy cooked crabs and lobsters at the Fishery shed, but do remember that the foreshore hereabouts is private.

Returning to the Colne river buoyage, red can buoys mark the mud spits formed by the small creeks which enter the river N and S of Rat Island. Above Rat Island the channel continues in a NNW'ly direction before turning NE'ly round Aldboro Point. Two red cans and a green conical buoy mark the course of the channel round this bend.

Alresford Creek

Fingringhoe Marshes, a nature reserve controlled by the Essex Naturalist Trust, are now on the port hand and a disused jetty will come into view on the same shore. The next buoy (green conical) will be found off the entrance to Alresford Creek. For a quarter of a mile inside the creek there are small boat moorings up to a ford at which landing can be made on either bank. From the ford up to Thorington Mill at the head of the creek is a little over a mile, but most of the creek dries out at LW. Out in the river there is enough water for large boats to lie afloat at LW out of the channel opposite Aldboro Point.

Above Alresford Creek the channel continues in a northerly direction and is well marked with both lit and unlit buoys round the sweeping bend known as Marriages Bight. The mud flat extending from the Finginghoe shore is extensive and the narrowing channel leads right over to within half a cable of the pleasantly wooded Alresford shore, before turning NW'ly again towards the other bank.

The last two channel buoys located just below the ballast quay on the Fingringhoe shore, are numbered 27 and 29 and both are green conical with flashing green lights. Above this point best water lies roughly midway between the banks.

By now the tidal barrier will be seen; it is normally open and therefore causes no problem. If 3FR(vert) lights show on the N pier, up or downstream, either the gates are shut or a large vessel is negotiating the barrier.

An aerial view of Brightlingsea – the village is on the left and the yacht moorings in the creek bending around to the south of Cindery Island

The riverfront at Wivenhoe on the Colne, with the tidal barrier downstream in the foreground

Port Guide: Wivenhoe	
Water	From quayside hose
Fuel	Diesel from yard. Petrol from garage ¾mile
Stores	Local shops including PO. EC Thurs
Repairs	By yard. Crane 3 tons
Chandler	At yard
Transport	Train service to Colchester and London
Club	Wivenhoe Sailing Club

Wivenhoe

The river front at Wivenhoe has a pleasant and unusual atmosphere, especially at high water with the sun shining on the quayside houses. All the large boats at Wivenhoe dry out at about half-ebb, when they settle in soft mud with their bows towards the quay.

Across the river from Wivenhoe is the entrance to Fingringhoe Creek or the Roman River – a reminder that the Romans settled in these parts nineteen centuries ago.

A ferry service sometimes runs between Rowhedge, Fingringhoe and Wivenhoe during the summer.

Rowhedge

Up-river on the W bank is Rowhedge, another little riverside town that some yachtsmen will have heard of because it was here that Alain Gerbault's famous *Firecrest* was built in 1892. Access to the quay at Rowhedge is possible from about two hours before and 1½ hours after HW.

It is unwise, and above Fingringhoe quay it is prohibited,

Port Guide: Rowhedge	
Water	From quayside hose
Diesel fuel	From garage
Stores	Local shops including PO

to anchor in the channel because of the commercial traffic to and from Colchester.

The remaining three miles of river between Rowhedge and the road bridge above the Hythe at Colchester should only be attempted after about four hours of flood. The best water, which will vary from 2m to 3m at the top of the tide, will generally be found midway between the banks. At night, during HW, one bank is lit by a continuous line of 'street lamps'.

Colchester

Berths alongside the quays at the Hythe dry out entirely and the barges and coasters using the port take the mud while they are there. The Hythe is not a good place to lie overnight, as ships may leave or arrive on the tide and there is very little room for them to manoeuvre.

While Colchester offers no special facilities for the yachtsman, all kinds of supplies are available there.

Colchester
Harbourmaster (01206) 827316, or VHF Ch 68.
Tidal information available around HW times

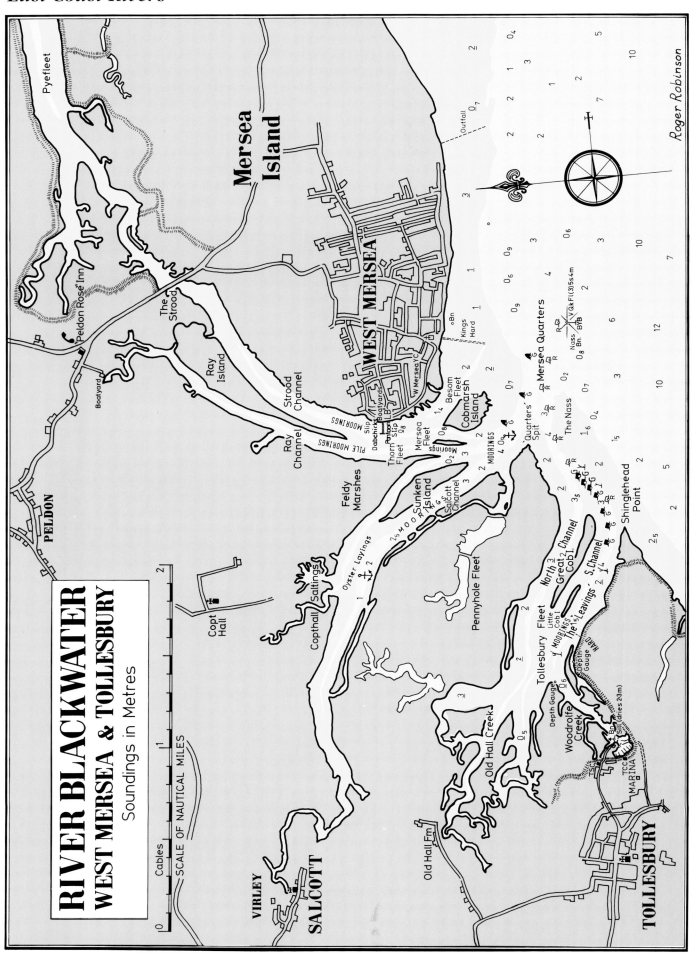

RIVER BLACKWATER
WEST MERSEA & TOLLESBURY
Soundings in Metres

Roger Robinson

10. The River Blackwater

Tides (Nass Beacon): HW Dover + 00.30 Range: Springs 4.6m Neaps 2.6m (HW Maldon approx 25 mins after HW West Mersea)
Charts: Admiralty 3741, Stanford No 4, Imray Y17
Waypoints: Bench Head Buoy 51.44.66N 01.01.20E. Nass Beacon 51.45.75N 00.54.88E
Hazard: Thirslet Spit

Arnold Bennett owned a Dutch barge-yacht called Velsa which he kept in Walton Backwaters but also sailed to Holland and other Essex and Suffolk rivers. In the Log of the Velsa he wrote: *'Time was when I agreed with the popular, and the guide book, verdict that the Orwell is the finest estuary in these parts; but now I know better. I unhesitatingly give the palm to the Blackwater. It is a noble stream, a true arm of the sea; its moods are more various, its banks wilder, and its atmospheric effects much grander. The season for cruising on the Blackwater is September, when the village regattas take place and the sunrises over leagues of marsh are made wonderful by strange mists.'*

The entrance to both the Blackwater and the Colne is generally considered to be at the Bench Head buoy, some 15 miles down-river from Maldon. Coming up from the south, most yachts follow the example of the sailing barges and go through the Swin Spitway.

The deepest water through this swatch is in a line between the Swin Spitway buoy, a safewater pillar buoy with spherical topmark (Iso 10s Bell), to the SE of the swatch, and the Wallet Spitway buoy (Sph R W V S LFl 10s Bell), a mile away to the NNW. Quite often a yacht gets a fair wind through the spitway when entering the Blackwater, but if ever it is necessary to beat through, then very short boards and constant use of the sounder are essential because the water shoals on to the Buxey Sands on the one hand and the Gunfleet Sands on the other.

From the Spitway, course is changed to bring the Knoll buoy (N Car B Y VQ) close to port after about two miles. Then, about a mile away is the Eagle (Con G Q G); to be passed close to starboard. With Eagle abeam, the red can of the NW Knoll light buoy (Can R Fl(2) R 5s) will usually be visible and is passed close to port. Then without altering course appreciably the unlit conical green Bench Head buoy can be left to starboard at the entrance to the Blackwater.

With the Bench Head astern, a newcomer will find it difficult to identify anything, except the conspicuous Nuclear Power Station at Bradwell, but a course of 295°M from the Bench Head will lead to the Nass beacon. This course is in fairly deep water – for the East Coast at least – and when the tide is running up against a westerly wind it is easy to tell where the channel lies because of the rougher water. After a while St Peter's Chapel should become visible on Sales Point to the SW, and at about the same time the trees and higher ground at West Mersea will take shape. The safest course is roughly midway between these two shores.

The Nass beacon, marking the entrance to Mersea Quarters, is a yellow and black steel post topped by a windmill generator and a quick flashing light, so that it is often easier to find by night than by day. There is little water near the Nass beacon – perhaps no more than 2m at LWS.

West Mersea

West Mersea is probably the most popular sailing centre on the River Blackwater and consequently it tends to be crowded. As at Brightlingsea, there are mooring piles in the Ray Channel and two boats can lie between each pair of posts; but beware of any submerged ropes. Visitors can moor temporarily between piles 1 and 2, while seeking a more permanent berth; the West Mersea Yacht Club boatman can usually advise. The deeper water is along the Mersea side of the piles.

It is risky to drop anchor anywhere but in the Quarters because of the many moorings farther in. In any case no yachtsman may anchor or go aground on any of the several oyster beds hereabouts. The principal oyster layings are in Mersea Fleet, running between Cob Marsh Island and Packing Marsh Island, and in the Salcott Channel leading out of the Quarters and up to the little villages of Salcott and Virley. Space has become so scarce at Mersea that moorings have now been laid well inside Salcott Creek.

Port Guide: West Mersea	
WMYC	Boatman VHF Ch 37 call sign YC ONE or mobile 0976 962178
Water	Standpipes at both ends of pontoon landing
Stores	Small shop at top of pontoon, and W. Mersea village EC Wed
Fuel	Diesel near top of pontoon, petrol in village
Repairs	Two yards with cranes; marine engineer; chandlery; sailmakers nearby.
Scrubbing posts	On foreshore (contact WMYC)
Transport	Buses to Colchester whence trains to London
Clubs	West Mersea YC (restaurant and bar weekends, and lunchtimes during week) Tel: 01206 382947 Dabchicks SC
Telephone	Near Victory Inn on Coast Road

The West Mersea Yacht Club – on the left – seen from the moorings in the Thornfleet at West Mersea

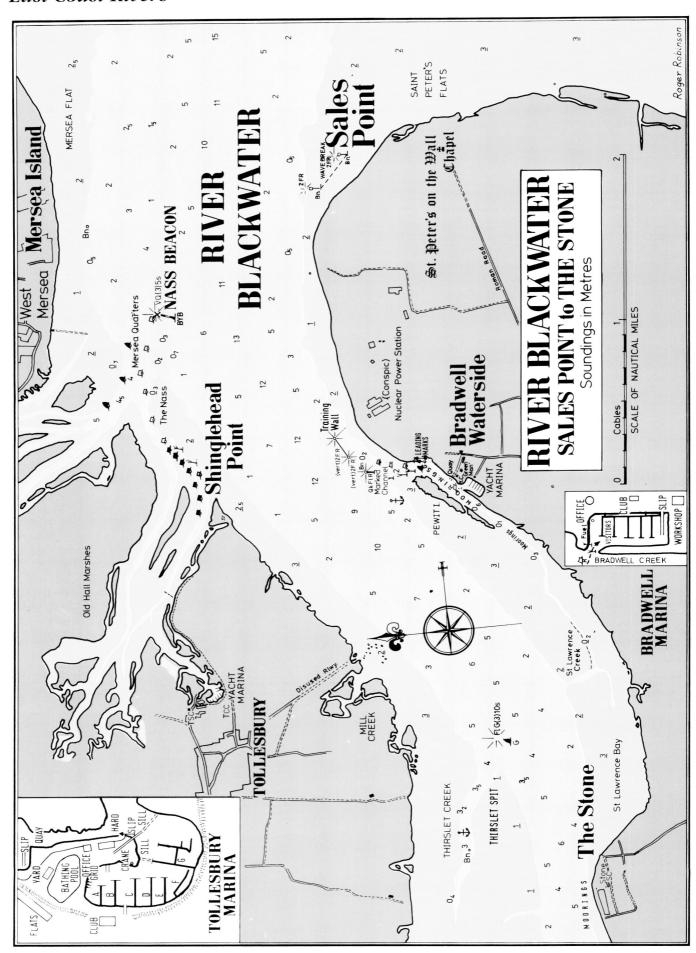

Mersea Island

West Mersea

MERSEA FLAT

MERSEA FLAT

Bn ○

RIVER BLACKWATER

Sales Point

SAINT PETER'S FLATS

WAVE BREAK
2FR
Bn □
2FR
Bn □

St. Peter's on the Wall Chapel

Roman Road

NASS BEACON
VQ(3)5s
BYB

Mersea Quarters

The Nass

(Conspic)
Nuclear Power Station

Shinglehead Point

Training Wall

(vert)2FR
Bn □
(vert)2FR
QkFl R
Marked Channel

Bradwell Waterside

LEADING MARKS

Quay
Hard

YACHT MARINA

M O O R I N G S

PEWIT I.

**RIVER BLACKWATER
SALES POINT to THE STONE**
Soundings in Metres

Cables
SCALE OF NAUTICAL MILES

OFFICE ○
Fuel
VISITORS
CLUB □
SLIP □
WORKSHOP
BRADWELL CREEK

Old Hall Marshes

Disused Rlwy.

MILL CREEK

Moorings

BRADWELL MARINA

St Lawrence Creek

YACHT MARINA
TCC
TSC

TOLLESBURY

FlG(3)10s
G

THIRSLET CREEK

Bn.
THIRSLET SPIT

The Stone

St Lawrence Bay

Stone SC

MOORINGS

TOLLESBURY MARINA

FLATS
SLIP
QUAY
YARD
HARD
SLIP
CRANE
SILL
SILL
OFFICE
GRID
BATHING POOL
CLUB
A B C D E F G

Roger Robinson

When moored in the Quarters it is a long way in to the pontoon landing at West Mersea, but quite often the club or yard boatman will take you ashore.

Tollesbury

Tollesbury Creek leads directly out of Mersea Quarters, and soon divides into the South Channel, which holds the more water, and the North Channel, with the Cob Islands between.

A red can indicates the junction of the Creek with the Quarters and this is followed by a further series of red cans up to the spit extending from Great Cob Island. The E Cardinal buoy marking this spit was missing in 1997, but the entrance to the South Channel is indicated by the first of a series of green cans (which sometimes appear blue). Keep close to these until you reach a line of moorings, which, together with port-hand withies show the best water up to the entrance of Woodrolfe Creek, marked by the first of four pairs of red and green cans. There is a tide gauge showing the depth of water over the sill at the yacht harbour.

Port Guide: Tollesbury	
Tollesbury Marina	Tel: 01621 868471
Water	On pontoons
Stores	Shops in village 10 minute walk. EC Wed
Fuel	Diesel and gas at yard
Chandlery	At yard
Repairs	3 slipways, lifts, cranage, workshops
Transport	Bus to Colchester rail station
Club	Tollesbury Cruising Club (in marina) Tel: 01621 869202 Tollesbury SC

If not intending to enter the marina, the best place to remain afloat is off the entrance to Woodrolfe Creek where there are several visitors' moorings belonging to Woodrolfe Boatyard. There is a hard just SE of the entrance to the creek and from there it is about a mile along the sea wall to the yacht harbour.

Tollesbury Marina

Keep to the centre of Woodrolfe Creek and the yacht harbour entrance will be seen south of the prominent white building of Woodrolfe Boatyard. Having entered the basin, moor temporarily at the jetty beneath the crane. While in the yacht harbour, visiting yachtsmen are welcome at Tollesbury Cruising Club where facilities include a swimming pool, tennis courts and restaurant

At HWS there is some 2m over the sill, but only about 1.5m at neaps.

On leaving the Quarters and rounding the Nass into the deep water of the Blackwater, the course when proceeding up to Osea Island or Maldon is approximately 250°M. Frequently, quite large ships are laid up in the main channel between the Mersea and Bradwell shores.

Bradwell Creek

About a mile up-river from the Nass, on the south shore is Bradwell Creek. The entrance is difficult to see but is in fact only about a quarter of a mile SW of the Barrier wall off the Nuclear Power Station.

Entrance to the creek is marked by a substantial beacon bearing a tide gauge that shows what water there is over the sill into the marina. Because the beacon is considered to be a port hand mark in the river Blackwater, its light flashes red.

From the beacon a line of red can buoys indicates the port

An aerial view of West Mersea showing the pontoon landing and, in the foreground, the pile moorings which are available for visiting yachts

An aerial view of Woodrolfe Creek looking up towards Tollesbury Marina at its head. The lightship is operated as a residential centre by the Fellowship Afloat Charitable Trust, which owns the saltmarshes

side of the gutway and a line of withies marks the other side. Best water will be found near the withies.

When the last of the can buoys has been left to port, the channel changes direction towards the SE, as indicated by two orange-painted triangular topped leading marks that will be seen rather low down in the saltings under a concrete slabbed section of the sea wall. After steering on these beacons for about a cable, the last mark – a green conical buoy – should be left to starboard before continuing along the line of moored craft that extends past the quay. A pair of red cans mark the end of a concrete slip near the quay end.

At the quay itself, there are still a few of the gnarled old tree-trunk piles to remind us of the days when the creek was always busy with sailing barges, loading from the farms around. There are still two scrubbing posts in use. They were erected by the Bradwell Quay YC who are quite willing for

visitors to use them provided they book a time and pay a small fee to the club.

The Essex County Council have based their Field Studies and Sailing Centre here at Bradwell Waterside, and there is usually a good deal of youthful activity as a result.

Bradwell Marina

The entrance to the marina is indicated by a red can buoy – 'Bradwell Marina' and the way in is marked by withies on either hand. Depths in the marina are slightly more than in the creek. Once inside, a visitor should berth on the ends of pontoons 'A' or 'B'.

The village of Bradwell (Bradwell Juxta-Mare) is about a mile from the quay and the Chapel of St Peter, probably the oldest building in England from which Christianity was preached, is another mile away along a track towards the sea.

Thirslet Creek

Out in the river again, the next thing to watch for is the green buoy (Fl(3)G 10s) marking a spit of hard sand which protrudes into the river on the north side at the entrance to Thirslet Creek.

Until the buoy is located, there is nothing to indicate how far into the river the spit extends, and many yachts have sailed headlong on to the hard sand while heading, as they thought, straight up the middle of the river. When coming down-river, a safe course results from steering on Bradwell Power Station. Although the water is deepest along this northern shore, the sand is dangerously steep-to, and care must therefore be taken not to stand over too far. It is safer to keep well over to the south shore until abreast St Lawrence Bay.

A couple of miles above Thirslet Creek, also amid the northern flats, is the entrance to Goldhanger Creek, marked by a conical green buoy. This also serves as a main river channel

Port Guide: Bradwell	
Marina	Tel: 01621 776235
	VHF Ch 37 or 80
Water	In Marina or from Bradwell
	Quay YC. (Near top of Hard)
Stores	Shop in village
Fuel	Diesel and petrol at marina
Chandler	At Marina
Repairs	At Marina. Slip up to 35 tons
Transport	Railway station Southminster;
	buses to Maldon; taxis
Telephone	Quarter of a mile from quay
Meals	Restaurant at marina, Green Man PH
	nearby, others in village
Clubs	Bradwell Cruising Club (Marina).
	Bradwell Quay Yacht Club.
	(Visitors welcome)

Port Guide: Maylandsea Bay	
Blackwater Marina	Tel: 01621 740264 VHF Ch 37
Water	From pontoons at yard
Stores	Several shops few minutes walk from yard
Fuel	At yard
Repairs	Yard with slipways, hoists, workshops
Chandler	At yard
Transport	Buses to Maldon and Chelmsford
Telephone	At marina clubhouse
Clubs	Maylandsea Bay Yacht Club; Harlow Sailing Club
Restaurant/bar	Blackwater Marina

The latest Thirslet Spit buoy, which replaced the previous green pillar buoy in 1997

buoy and must, therefore, be left to port when entering the creek. The creek leads up to a hard near Goldhanger village, but this can really only be reached by dinghy since there is very little water at the head of the creek, even at HWS.

But for those who appreciate the quiet of remote anchorages, there is enough water in which to lie afloat overnight for half a mile or more within the entrances to both Thirslet and Goldhanger Creeks. There is a reasonably hard foreshore near the top of Goldhanger Creek and a path along the sea wall can be used to reach the village, a mile or so away. There are oyster layings in the creek.

Stone St Lawrence

Over on the south shore is Stone St Lawrence, easily located by the many boats moored in the bay and bungalows and caravans on shore. Landing from a dinghy is possible on the shingly beach at all states of the tide. Water can be obtained from the clubhouse of the Stone Sailing Club, and a few simple provisions may be found nearby.

Another club (Marconi SC) has its clubhouse half a mile farther up-river and at night a fixed yellow light is shown from a corner of the building. There are four rows of moorings, and one for visitors opposite the club; water is at the top of the slip.

From St Lawrence Bay the remains of the little pier at Osea Island can be seen in daylight and its two fixed green lights at night. It is safe for any but deep draught boats to set a course direct to the end of the pier. Larger boats must watch out for a shallow patch known as the Barnacle just east of the pier.

Osea Island

The southern side of Osea Island has been used as an anchorage for centuries. Almost certainly the longboats of the Vikings lay there before the battle of Maldon in 991AD and throughout the 19th century collier brigs would have waited off the island for water to take them up to the Hythe at Maldon.

Lawling Creek and Maylandsea

Half a mile or so across the river from Osea lies Lawling Creek, the entrance to which is marked by a red can (Fl 3s). Once over the shallow bar (1m LWS) and past the yellow Blackwater Marina buoy, there are some small red and green spar buoys, but more useful are the mooring buoys showing a letter 'C' that have been laid in the middle of the channel. A yacht can reach the yard for about half the tide, but in a dinghy it is possible at almost any time. As well as the many swinging moorings that extend throughout the length of the creek, the yard has serviced floating pontoons and three slipways. All forms of repair and rigging can be undertaken and there is a launch service available.

It is a good thing for yachtsmen that the Maldon District Council buoy the Blackwater above Osea Island, because the channel follows a much less obvious course in the upper reaches of the river. Just above the remains of Osea pier a green conical buoy guards a mudbank known as the Doctor. Above the Doctor the channel turns to the NW, past a port hand red can buoy. If a boat draws four or five feet, this is about as far up-river as she can expect to reach and remain afloat at LW. Two more buoys – one a green conical (Fl G 3s) and the other a red can – known locally as the 'Doubles', are located just above the entrance to Southey Creek.

By this time a rather long, low, white building should be seen about a mile ahead. This is the clubhouse of the Blackwater SC and it will serve as a mark on which to steer until the red can buoy marking Hilly Pool Point at the northern end of Northey Island is seen to port. A light (Iso G 5s) is shown from the roof of the Blackwater SC.

After rounding the Point and turning sharply southwards into Collier's Reach, the cluster of houses round Heybridge Lock will come into view about half a mile away. It is never very easy to tell whether the lock gates are open or shut until close to and in line with them, but if it is necessary to wait, there is good holding ground in the river outside the lock.

From an hour before to an hour after high water a boat

Port Guide: Heybridge Basin	
Lockmaster	Tel: 01621 853506
Water	Stand pipe near inner lock gates
Stores	Limited supply from chandler
Chandlery	
Fuel	Near Lock
Transport	Infrequent buses to Maldon (whence good connections)
Telephone	110 yards from lock
Repairs	Slip outside lock
Club	Blackwater SC (Est 1899) quarter mile from lock

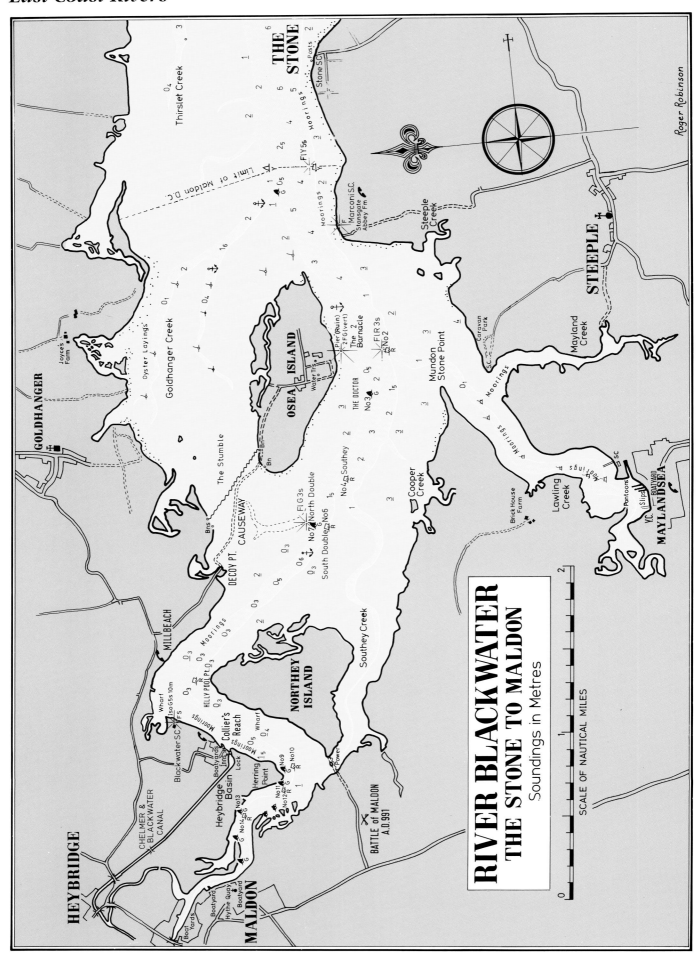

THE STONE

Thirslet Creek

Stone S.C.

Limit of Maldon D.C.

FlY5s

Moorings

Marconi S.C.
Stansgate
Abbey Fm

Steeple Creek

STEEPLE

Mayland Creek

Caravan Park

S.C.

Moorings

GOLDHANGER

Joyce's Farm

Oyster Layings

Goldhanger Creek

OSEA ISLAND

Water Trs

Pier (Ruin)
2FG(vert)
The 2 Barnacle

Fl R 3s
No2 R

Mundon Stone Point

The Stumble

Bn

Bn

THE DOCTOR

No3 G

No4 R Southey R

South Double No6 R

Cooper Creek

Brick House Farm

Lawling Creek

Pontoons

Slips

Y.C.   BOATYARD

SC

MAYLANDSEA

DECOY PT.

CAUSEWAY

Fl G 3s

No7 R North Double

MILLBEACH

Moorings

HILLY POOL Pt.

Wharf
Iso6s10m FS

Blackwater S.C.

Mooring s

Collier's Reach

NORTHEY ISLAND

Wharf

Southey Creek

Power

CHELMER & BLACKWATER CANAL

Inn

Boatyards

Heybridge Basin

Lock

Moorings

Herring Point

No1 R

No11 R

No12 G No9 G

No10 R

No13 G

No14 G

HEYBRIDGE

Boatyard

Hythe Quay

Boatyard

Boat Yards

MALDON

BATTLE of MALDON A.D.991

RIVER BLACKWATER
THE STONE TO MALDON
Soundings in Metres

SCALE OF NAUTICAL MILES

Roger Robinson

Heybridge Basin and the Chelmer and Blackwater Navigation Canal were constructed in 1797. The bridges and locks were designed by Rennie and the 14 miles of cannal end in Chelmsford. A licence is necessary for boats navigating the canal. The Basin is managed by the Chelmer and Blackwater Navigation Co (with offices at 10 Bradford Street, Braintree).

From off the entrance to the lock, the river continues in a south-westerly direction for about a quarter of a mile before turning N round Herring Point. From here up to Maldon the winding channel is well marked with conical green buoys on the starboard and red cans on the port hand. Apart from one or two holes, the river dries out completely at Maldon, and most of the boats take the mud, either alongside a floating pontoon near the Town Quay, or off the yard next to it. Visiting yachts may berth temporarily afloat or for longer periods if prepared to take the ground.

As you pass the western end of Northey Island, give a thought to the heroic defence of Maldon by Brythnoth's men against the Danes a thousand years ago.

Colloryan

Heybridge Basin, looking towards the lock, the Old Ship Inn can be seen on the right

drawing six or seven feet should have no great difficulty in getting into or out of Heybridge Lock. Because of the need to retain water in the canal during the summer months, the lock is worked for only one hour before HW during neap tides. At springs the lock will be worked over a longer period. Prior notification and confirmation is required if the lock is to be used at night.

Port Guide: Maldon
Maldon Quay River

Bailiff	Tel: 01621 856487
Water	At quayside and boatyards
Stores	Many shops in town. EC Wed
Fuel	From pumps at yard pontoon
Repairs	Two yards with slipways
Sailmaker	Near quayside
Transport	Bus to Chelmsford rail station
Clubs	Maldon YC. Maldon Little Ship Club
VHF	The yard keeps a listening watch on Ch 37

Around the top of the tide, yachts can lie afloat alongside the Town Quay at Maldon

11. The River Crouch

Tides (Burnham on Crouch): HW Dover + 1.10 Range: Springs 5.0m Neaps 3.2m (HW at Whitaker Beacon approx 20 mins before HW at Burnham)

Charts: Admiralty 3750, Stanford No 4, Imray Y15

Waypoints: Wallet Spitway Buoy 51.42.83N 01.07.42E Swin Spitway Buoy 51.41.92N 01.08.45E
Whitaker Bell Buoy 51.41.40N 01.10.61E Whitaker Beacon 51.39.62N 01.06.30E
Ridge Buoy 51.40.10N 01.05.00E Sunken Buxey Buoy 51.39.50N 01.00.70E
Outer Crouch Buoy 51.38.35N 00.58.61E Buxey Beacon 51.41.13N 01.01.38E

Hazard: Shoal water between Swin Spitway and Whitaker Beacon

Some people say Burnham's popularity as a sailing centre has declined recently, but if you arrive in the Crouch during Burnham Week, you'll be thankful the place is no more popular than it already is.

As a river, the Crouch can hardly be described as beautiful. Its higher reaches are certainly more pleasant than the five or six miles between Burnham and Shore Ends, where nothing much can be seen above the bordering sea walls except for a short while at high tide. Yet because of these unobstructed shores, the Crouch offers racing yachtsmen the best possible sport, and with the smaller river Roach entering at right angles, a variety of courses can be laid to suit all wind conditions.

Buoyage of River Crouch

In 1987 Trinity House handed over responsibility for the buoyage and marking of the River Crouch to the Crouch Harbour Authority. The commercial user of the river is a company importing and landing timber at Baltic Wharf.

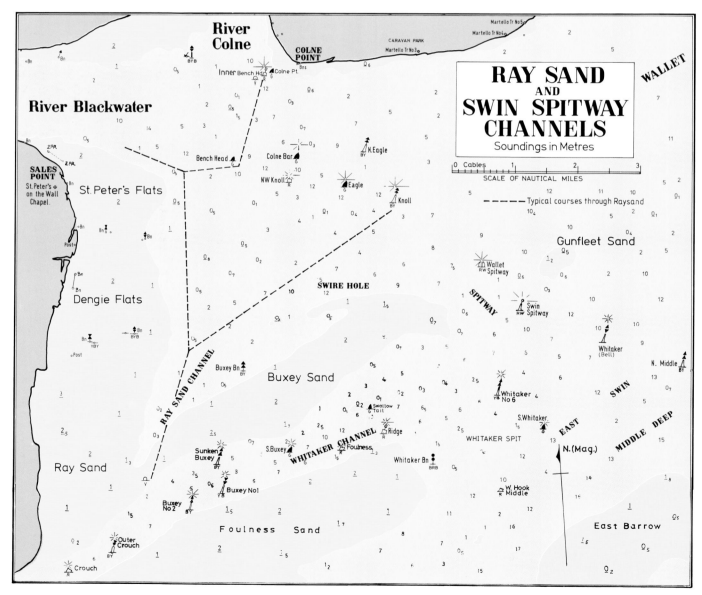

The waterfront at Burnham-on-Crouch. The ferry, which runs to Wallasea on the south bank, is on the right

In 1988 the Harbour Authority came to an arrangement with the commercial interests as to the number and type of buoys necessary to allow navigation of the river at any time. As a consequence all the buoys in the river were lit. However, the amount of shipping using the river subsequently declined and some of the buoys were removed in 1992. The wharf is now under new ownership (1997) and in future, traffic may increase from one to two ships a week.

From Battlesbridge, the navigable limit of the river, down to Shore Ends where the Crouch clears the land, is approximately 15 miles. From Shore Ends out to the Whitaker bell buoy marking the extremity of the Whitaker Spit as another nine or ten miles.

Excluding the top-of-the-tide entrance through Havengore Creek and the river Roach, there are two approaches to the Crouch: through the Whitaker Channel from the Swin or the Spitway and through the very shallow Ray Sand (Rays'n) Channel between Dengie Flats and the Buxey Sands. The deep water approach will be considered first.

When coming S through the Swin Spitway, shape a course of 200°M (towards Whitaker No 6 buoy) from the Spitway buoy until the Ridge buoy (red can with topmark) bears 255°M before changing on to that bearing to pass just N of the Ridge buoy itself. From the Ridge and Foulness buoys, a course should be set to Buxey No 1 buoy, leaving the S Buxey (conical green) buoy to starboard.

The channel between the Ridge and Swallow Tail is wide and deep, but the channel to the north of the Swallow Tail is often used when sailing between the Spitway and S. Buxey buoys.

Both sides of the Sunken Buxey shoal are now marked and many yachtsmen prefer to pass to the south of the shoal, leaving the S Cardinal, Buxey No 1 (VQ(6)L Fl 10s) buoy to starboard and the N Cardinal Buxey No 2 (FlR 10s) to port. This way in is probably easier with a fair wind or under power, but when beating, the northern side of the shoal will allow longer boards.

When coming from the S, round the Whitaker Beacon, deep water will be found about midway between Whitaker No 6 (N Cardinal) and the Ridge buoy and when the latter bears 255°M, change onto that course. Once the Outer Crouch buoy (S Cardinal Q(6) + LFl 15s) has been located, course should be shaped to leave it close to starboard and thence into the river.

The Raysand Channel

Moderate draught yachts bound from the Blackwater to the Crouch can, at the right state of the tide, come through the Ray Sand or Rays'n Channel. There is little or no water in the southern end of the swatchway at LWS, in fact it is possible at low water extraordinary springs to walk virtually dry footed from the mainland to the Buxey Sands.

The time honoured Buxey Beacon still stands where it did when Maurice Griffiths wrote The Magic of the Swatchways, but no longer with its easily recognised sign-post topmark. Instead, a N Cardinal mark tops the beacon, which, like the Whitaker, now has a tripod base. Trinity House has now disowned this and several other beacons in the Thames Estuary, so we must hope that local authorities or yacht clubs will see that they are maintained in future.

The Dengie Flats were once used as a dive-bombing range and four derelict target craft still remain as a reminder. These wrecks are marked by unlit beacons; the two inshore having W Cardinal topmarks and the outer two with E Cardinal topmarks.

When bound from the Wallet past the Knoll buoy, the best course to hold into the Rays'n will be 235°M. The N Buxey buoy is no longer there to guide you, but sudden changes in depth near the Swire Hole should serve to locate you on the chart. When the Buxey Beacon bears 180°M, change course to 215°M to pass it about half a mile away to port.

Finally, when the conspicuous pylons on Foulness Island come to bear 210°M, change on to this course until the deeper water of the Crouch is found – about a mile to the W of the Sunken Buxey buoy, with its double cone (N Cardinal) topmark.

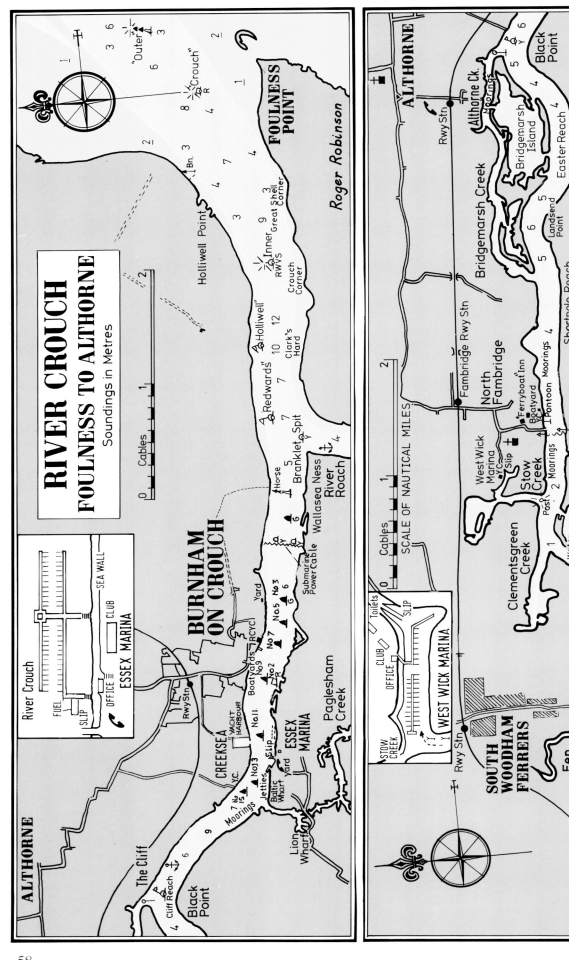

RIVER CROUCH
FOULNESS TO ALTHORNE
Soundings in Metres

RIVER CROUCH
ALTHORNE TO BATTLESBRIDGE
Soundings in Metres

Shallow draught boats, using a rising tide, can often sneak through the Rays'n closer inshore by following a course approximately 185°M and about a mile to seaward of the outer pair of wrecked target vessels. This is the area in which to change course to about N, if bound from the Crouch to the Blackwater.

A small spherical yellow buoy is laid in the S entrance to the Rays'n by the Burnham yacht clubs and is intended to indicate a way through the swatch. There is a shallow patch to the west of this buoy, which is best treated as an east mark. Even so, do not expect to find any clear cut channel or gutway.

About one and a half miles SW of the Outer Crouch buoy and just inside the river itself is the Crouch red can buoy (Fl R 10s). After the Crouch buoy direction is changed to a westerly course, which can be held up-river as far as the junction of the river Roach about three miles away. Half-way between the Crouch buoy and the entrance to the Roach is the Sph RW 'Inner Crouch' (L Fl W 10s), which can be passed on either hand. Two racing buoys may be seen on the northern side of the channel, just below the entrance to the Roach, and these should be left to the north to be sure of missing the mud of Redward Flats. The Branklet Spit buoy (Spher Y) marks an arm of mud that extends north-easterly from Wallasea Ness. West of Branklet Spit deepest water is to be found near the N bank of the river; but because the south shore is steep-to, it is often the safer one to work.

A North Cardinal buoy 'Horse' (Q Fl) just above the entrance to the river Roach, was originally intended to mark the S end of a dredged channel leading to the Burnham Fairway buoy; but it is doubtful whether the channel still remains.

The many yacht moorings off Burnham commence just above a group of four yellow spherical buoys marking submerged cables carrying 33,000 volts. The Burnham Fairway is on the S side of the river and although narrow, it is well marked by eight starboard-hand buoys (QG) and one port-hand can buoy (QR). There is at least 4 m of water throughout the length of the Fairway and the south shore is steep-to. When it becomes necessary to beat up-river and boards on the

Port Guide: Burnham-on-Crouch Crouch	
Harbourmaster Launch	Tel: 01621 783602 Mon-Fri am VHF Ch 80
Burnham Yacht Harbour	Tel: 01621 782150 VHF Ch 80
Water	Yacht harbour and stand-pipes near most landing places
Stores	Shops in main street. EC Wed
Fuel	Diesel from yacht harbour, petrol in town
Repairs	Shipwrights and marine engineers along waterfront. Slipway, 30 ton hoist, engineers at yacht harbour
Chandlery	On quay and at yacht harbour
Sailmakers	In town and at yacht harbour
Meals	Restaurants in town and at yacht clubs
Transport	Train service to London via Wickford except on Sundays in winter months. (Station 15 minutes walk)
Clubs	Royal Corinthian Yacht Club (01621 782105) Royal Burnham Yacht Club (782044). Crouch Yacht Club (782252) Burnham Sailing Club
Telephone	Near White Hart

port tack are extended in among the moored craft, a close watch should be kept on the effects of the tide, for the ebb at spring tides can run at 3 knots past Burnham.

Anchoring is obviously prohibited in the Fairway and the multitude of moorings makes it very difficult to bring up to an anchor anywhere in the area. The Royal Corinthian Yacht Club has a visitor's mooring sited directly off their conspicuous clubhouse, but if this is occupied, enquiries will usually lead to the provision of some other vacant buoy.

There are four floating pontoons off the Burnham waterfront at which boats may lie for short periods while seeking supplies or services ashore. The pontoons belong to the Royal Corinthian YC, the Royal Burnham YC, Prior's boatyard and the Crouch YC.

Burnham Yacht Harbour, at the western end of the town, can be entered at all states of the tide. The entrance is marked by a yellow pillar buoy with X topmark (Fl Y 5s) and a couple of posts with red and green flashing lights.

The little town is a pleasant place, there are facilities for yachtsmen close at hand, and many of its people are in some way connected with sailing.

Wallasea Bay

On the opposite shore and about a mile up-river from Burnham is Wallasea Bay. Here again the moorings are numerous, but this time located along the S as well as the N side of the river. Many of the yachts at Wallasea Bay remain

The Horse Shoal, or number 1 buoy, originally marked the S end of a dredged channel to Burnham Fairway

Port Guide: Wallasea Bay	
Essex Marina	Tel: 01702 258531 VHF Ch 80
Water	From pontoon
Stores	Shop near boatyard
Fuel	Petrol and diesel from fuel barge
Chandler	Near yard
Repairs	Yard with slipway and crane
Meals	Restaurant nearby
Transport	Buses to Southend-on-Sea. W/E Ferry to Burnham in season.
Club	Wallasea Bay Yacht Club
Telephone	W end of sea wall

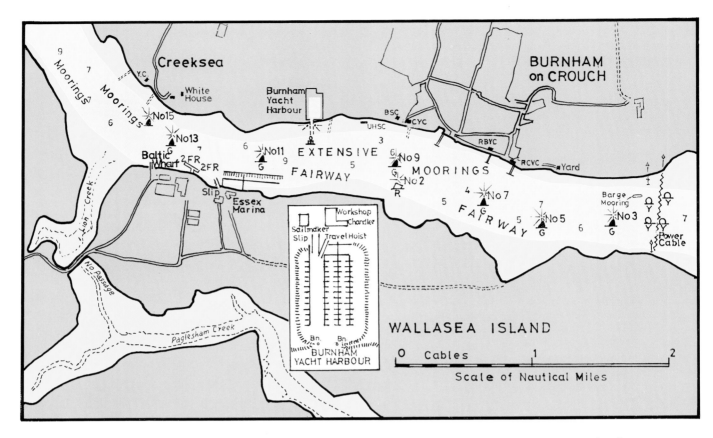

A lit, yellow, safe water buoy marks the entrance to Burnham Yacht Harbour. The green starboard-hand of the pair of entrance beacons can also be seen.

afloat along the outside of pontoons of a floating harbour in plenty of water at all states of the tide.

The Essex Marina has finger-berth pontoons and some pile berths have been established along with improved toilet, shower and laundry facilities.

The western end of Burnham Fairway is marked by the No 13 buoy off the Baltic timber wharf. There is shallow water on the north side of the river just below Creeksea.

The river now turns north-westerly through Cliff Reach; so called because of the modest (40-50ft) cliff just above Creeksea. Cliff reach is important to the yachtsman inasmuch as it provides shelter from south-westerly winds, when most of the other reaches in the Crouch are made uncomfortable. Towards low tide a good look-out should be kept for a line of concrete sinkers that can be found along the low water line below the cliff. At the top of Cliff Reach the main stream turns

south-westerly round Black Point, where the shore is steep-to, into Easter Reach. But a minor branch continues north-west.

Althorne Creek

A yellow racing buoy marked 'Cliff Reach' is usually located off Black Point, and it provides a mark for entering Althorne Creek.

The entrance to the creek is now marked by a port-hand beacon (with a red light) and a series of three red can buoys. The course when entering is roughly N (Mag), leaving the beacon and the first red can close to port.

At Bridgemarsh Marina (tel: 01621 740414) there are nearly hundred boats moored to pontoons between piles along the centre of the creek both above and below the point where there was once a ford leading on to Bridgemarsh Island. On the N bank there is a yard with two docks, a slipway and a crane. There is water, and power, to the pontoons, and toilet and showers are provided. Althorne station is only about a

The anchorage beneath the modest cliff just upriver from Creeksea in Cliff Reach

The floating pontoon at the North Fambridge Yacht Club

quarter of a mile away whence it is no more than an hour to Liverpool Street station in London.

It is possible in a small craft, with a rising tide and a commanding wind, to sail through Althorne Creek and Bridgemarsh Creek to join the Crouch again some two miles further up-stream; but the channel is extremely narrow and tortuous.

From the Cliff Reach buoy the river flows south-westerly through Easter Reach, where during the summer the last of the racing buoys – 'Canewdon' – is located in mid-stream in about 5 metres at LW. Then, from abreast the point where Bridgemarsh Creek emerges from behind the western end of the island, the river flows westerly for two or three miles straight through Shortpole and Longpole Reaches up to and beyond North and South Fambridge. There is no less than 4 metres of water in mid-channel up as far as North Fambridge.

North Fambridge

Francis B Cooke, whose many books on small boat cruising have become collectors' items, on the occasion of his hundredth birthday, contributed an autobiographical note entitled: 'Birth of a Great Yacht Station' to Yachting Monthly and in it he wrote: *'Anyone seeing Fambridge today for the first time could hardly imagine what a delightful waterside hamlet it was when I first discovered it (in 1893). The only buildings near the water were Fambridge Hall, the old Ferry Boat Inn, a tiny school, a row of four or five small timber built cottages, an old barn and the little church nestling among the trees. The road leading down to the Ferry hard was just a narrow country lane, with wild roses blooming in the summer. My friends the Viner brothers had decided to spend the summer there and asked me to join them. I readily agreed and we arranged with the*

landlady of the Ferry Boat Inn to board there. She agreed to take us for twelve shillings a week and hoped she was not charging too much, but of course that would include our laundry.'

There are four lines of moored boats off Fambridge with a fairway between them, so the only possible places to anchor are above or below these moorings. But there is plenty of water (2.5m) even at LWS.

Landing is possible on the hard, or at the floating pontoon near the clubhouse on the N Fambridge side. Landing on the S bank is not easy.

Stow Creek

Rather less than a mile above Fambridge, Stow Creek enters the river from the N side.

The entrance is marked with a Beacon on a pile, and this should be left close to starboard when entering. The creek is then marked (occasionally) with starboard hand withies up to the entrance to Westwick Marina, just over a quarter of a mile from the entrance. Here, boats lie to pontoons, in about 1m at LWS.

Above Stow Creek the river narrows and shallows fairly rapidly. Clementsgreen Creek is navigable only around HW, and since it is dammed it is of little interest to yachtsmen. From abreast this creek the river turns south-westerly through Brandy Hole reach into Brandy Hole Bay, which is a water-skiing area and very busy at weekends. Moorings begin again off Brandy Hole YC and continue for a mile or more up to the entrance to Fenn Creek, just above the ford at Hullbridge. Anywhere along here, a boat will take the ground for an hour or two either side of LW. Watch out for a spit extending from the N bank just above Brandy Hole YC.

There are two other yacht clubs on the S shore and one on the N bank near the road down to the ford.

Above Hullbridge the river becomes very narrow and tortuous, and in places is no more than 10 or 12m wide between the retaining walls, although there are some moorings in Long Reach. At springs, a boat drawing 2m can take the tide right up to Battlesbridge, but unless the return trip is commenced almost immediately, it would be best to moor alongside the concrete landing quay, or a small pontoon on the S bank.

HW at Hullbridge is 25 minutes later than at Burnham.

Port Guide: North Fambridge

North Fambridge Yacht Station	Tel: 01621 740370
West Wick Marina (Stow Creek)	Tel: 01621 741268
Water	Near boatshed at Yacht Station, on pontoons at marina
Stores	Shop and PO at N Fambridge (½ mile)
Fuel	TVO and diesel from yard, diesel at marina
Repairs	Slipway, crane, shipwright and chandlers
Transport	Trains to London from Fambridge station (1 mile) except on Sundays in winter months
Club	North Fambridge YC, West Wick YC
Meals	At Ferry Boat Inn

Port Guide: Hullbridge (Brandy Hole)

Brandy Hole Yacht Station	Tel: 01702 230248
Water	At hard and clubhouses
Stores	At Hullbridge village, or near Hullbridge YC
Fuel	Diesel at Brandy Hole Yacht Station, petrol at Garages (1 mile)
Repairs	Boatyard adjacent to Brandy Hole Yacht Club
Transport	Buses from Hullbridge to Southend (from The Anchor)
Clubs	Brandy Hole YC. Up River YC. Hullbridge YC. Woodham Ferrers YC

Port Guide: Battlesbridge

Water	From The Barge (by request)
Stores	Nearby (Many Antique shops)
Petrol and oil	Garage nearby
Transport	Trains to London from Battlesbridge station, except on Sundays in winter. Buses to Maldon and Southend

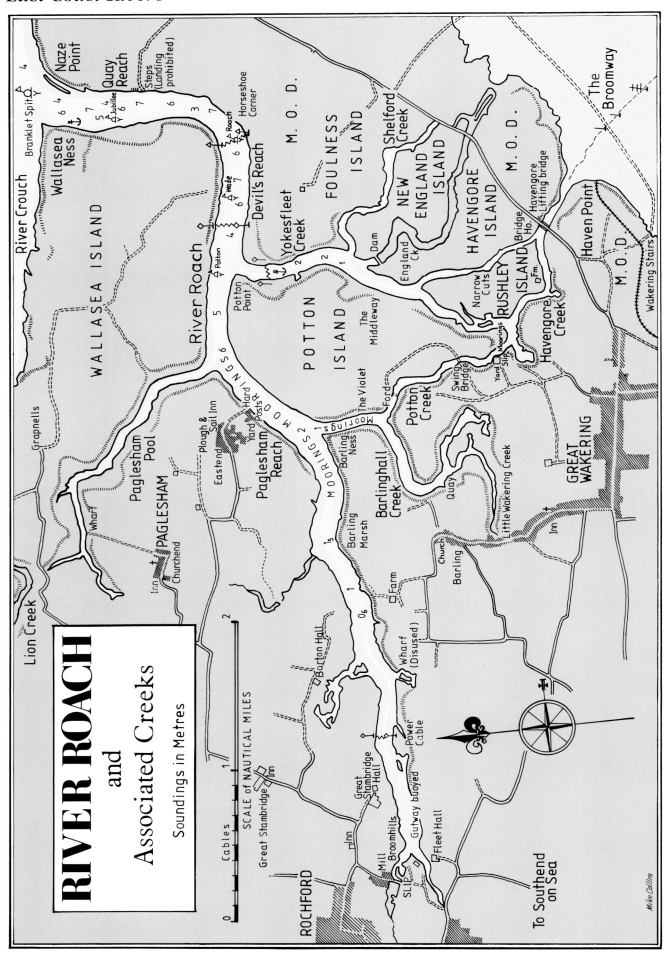

RIVER ROACH
and
Associated Creeks
Soundings in Metres

SCALE of NAUTICAL MILES

Cables

Mike Collins

ROCHFORD

To Southend on Sea

Lion Creek

River Crouch

Branklet Spit

Naze Point

Quay Reach

Steps (Landing prohibited)

Jubilee

Wallasea Ness

WALLASEA ISLAND

Horseshoe Corner

Roach

M. O. D.

Wade

Devil's Reach

River Roach

Yokesfleet Creek

FOULNESS ISLAND

Shelford Creek

M. O. D.

The Broomway

Potton Point

Potton

NEW ENGLAND ISLAND

Dam

England Ck.

HAVENGORE ISLAND

M. O. D.

Havengore Lifting bridge

Bridge Ho.

Haven Point

M. O. D.

Wakering Stairs

Grapnells

Paglesham Pool

Wharf

PAGLESHAM

Churchend

Inn

Plough & Sail Inn

Eastend

Yard

Hard

Posts

Paglesham Reach

POTTON ISLAND

The Middleway

The Violet

Ford

MOORINGS

Moorings

Narrow Cuts

RUSHLEY ISLAND

Fm.

Moorings

Slip

Yard

Swing Bridge

Havengore Creek

Potton Creek

Barling Ness

Barlinghall Creek

Barling Marsh

Quay

Little Wakering Creek

GREAT WAKERING

Church

Barling

Inn

Barton Hall

Farm

Wharf (Disused)

Power Cable

Great Stambridge Hall

Gutway buoyed

Fleet Hall

Mill

Broomhills

SLIP

Great Stambridge

Inn

Inn

12. The River Roach and Havengore

Tides (Paglesham): HW Dover + 1.10 Range: Springs 5.0m Neaps 3.2m
Charts: Admiralty 3750, Stanford No 4, Imray Y 17
Waypoints: Branklet Spit 51.36.95N 00.52.24E
East Shoebury Beacon 51.30.52N 00.53.99E
Hazard: Havengore route – except on rising tide

Those of us who are based on the Roach consider it to be a better river than the Crouch because its several changes of direction offer a wider variety of sailing and because its upper reaches have remained quite unspoilt. Another advantage is that Havengore is nearby to provide us with a 'back-door' to the Thames and Medway or even across the Estuary to the Foreland. From its junction with the River Crouch, about three miles inside Shore Ends, the Roach winds for some six miles in a mainly south-westerly direction up to its tidal limit at Stambridge Mill. Apart from the lower reaches below Paglesham, the Roach is very narrow at low water and not many craft use the river above Barling Ness.

What does make the Roach interesting to many yachtsmen is the network of subsidiary creeks which link the river with the sea over the Maplin Sands. The best-known and most important of these small channels is Havengore Creek, passing Havengore and Rushley Islands and through a lifting bridge at its eastern end. By using this creek after crossing the Maplins near HW, it is possible for small and shallow craft to reach the Roach without having to sail down the W Swin and up the Whitaker Channel.

At its mouth at HW the Roach is more than a quarter of a mile wide, but mud extends from both banks to reduce the LW channel to half that width. The mud extending from Wallasea Ness is marked by the Branklet Spit buoy (Spher Y). On the eastern side of the entrance much mud extends from Nase Point and many boats have been tripped up here.

Quay Reach

There is not much less than 6m at LW in the middle of the river right along Quay Reach. The direction of this lowest reach of the Roach is roughly N-S, and because of this it often provides a more comfortable berth than any anchorage in the Crouch below Creeksea. Not only is there good protection from westerly and easterly winds, but there is also plenty of room and good holding ground in stiff mud towards either shore. On the E shore there are some landing steps (very weedy and slippery) built into a small promontory in the seawall. It is possible, but not easy, to land here and walk to Church End where you may visit the pub and/or the church - the walk takes 30-40 minutes. Foulness is MOD property, so you must keep to the track.

From the entrance up to Horseshoe Corner at the southern end of Quay Reach is just over a mile; then the river turns

Looking up Paglesham Reach towards Barlingness from the old black shed at the boatyard

63

The scrubbing post and Shuttlewood's old black shed at the top of the hard at Paglesham

through more than a right angle to continue westerly into Devil's Reach. The deep water round this bend, known as Whitehouse Hole, is marked by a yellow racing buoy ('Roach') in about 6m at LW. The many, named, yellow buoys in the lower reaches of the Crouch and Roach from March to December are used by the Burnham yacht clubs' racing fleets.

The next racing buoy is 'Wade' (formerly 'Whitehouse') located farther up-river, after which the channel divides just below the 'Potton' buoy. The principal arm continues westerly along the northern side of Potton Island, leading to Paglesham Reach, while the other branch turns S, along the eastern side of Potton, into the Yokesfleet.

Paglesham Reach

Just before the moorings are reached in Paglesham Reach the main channel turns to the SW abreast the entrance to Paglesham Pool (or Creek). This narrow creek carries so little water at low tide as to be of little interest for navigation. At one time it was possible at HW to pass round the western side of Wallasea Island via Paglesham Pool and Lion Creek into the Crouch opposite Creeksea, but the roadway onto the island now separates the two creeks.

Just above the junction of Paglesham Pool with the Roach are the first of the Paglesham moorings, which extend both below and above Shuttlewood's old building shed. The moorings are laid on both sides of the channel, and the Crouch Harbour Board has laid port and starboard hand buoys to mark the extent of a fairway within which anchoring is now prohibited because of the commercial traffic that is trading at the quay near Stambridge Mill. Visiting yachtsmen are now advised to anchor just below the moorings off Paglesham Pool, whence a landing can be made near a 'pill box' on the sea wall. Alternatively craft with little draught or those that can take the ground, might sometimes be able to find an anchorage just outside the northern limit of the fairway. The hard has been widened, but boots of some kind are very desirable when landing.

Port Guide: Paglesham	
Diesel fuel and water	From yard
Stores	None
Repairs	Shipwright at top of hard
Transport	Buses from East End to Rochford, whence trains to London
Telephone	Near Plough and Sail at top of lane

A riding light is essential when anchored in the Roach overnight – the river is occasionally used by fishing vessels, and at high water by small freighters bound for Stambridge, by day or night.

The hamlet of East End, which yachtsmen usually think of as Paglesham, is about half a mile from the landing beside Shuttlewood's shed. Sadly, there is no longer a shop at East End, but there is food at the Plough and Sail.

Above the Paglesham moorings the river forks again at Barling Ness, the main stream continuing westerly towards Rochford and the other arm turning S between Barling Marsh and Potton Island. The continuation of the main channel west of Barling Ness is sometimes referred to as the Broomhill river. There is 1 to 1.5m of water at LWS up as far as disused Barling Quay on the S bank, after which the channel narrows rapidly into a gutway that can be navigated only towards HW, and then only with much sounding or local knowledge. At HW boats drawing 1 to 1.5m can continue as far upriver as the mill at Stambridge – a mile short of the town of Rochford. On the whole, best water will be found roughly midway between the banks in these upper reaches, but the broad entrance to Bartonhall Creek must be avoided on the N bank. A power cable crosses the river hereabouts and is marked by a green conical and a red can buoy.

Just below Stambridge Mill the river divides for the last time, the southern arm becoming Fleethall Creek where there is a wharf that is used by small freighters and a slipway capable of handling craft up to 60 tons and 70 ft LOA. However, this yard (Sutton Wharf) is not interested in taking boats smaller than 30ft LOA. Ships bringing grain to Stambridge Mill berth on the N side of the river just below the sluice gates, but yachts are not permitted to use the quay. The Wakering YC is now based just inside Fleet Hall Creek.

Yokesfleet Creek

Returning now to the S bank of the river, the branch of the Roach which turns S at Potton Point is variously know as Yokesfleet Creek and the Gore Channel. The entrance to this creek requires care as a spit of mud stretches out from Potton Point and there is also an extensive mud flat off the opposite point. Best water will be found close under the Potton or western shore for the first few cables inside. There are depths of about 2 metres at LW for the first quarter of a mile or so inside the creek, and the spot provides a quiet and comfortable anchorage during either W or E winds.

About a mile within Yokesfleet Creek two lesser creeks branch out on the eastern side. The first is Shelford Creek, which once reached the sea along the S side of Foulness Island; and the second, New England Creek, has been dammed just within its entrance. This barrier across New England Creek provides a useful reference point as it is at the next division of the main channel that Narrow Cuts leads off south-easterly towards Havengore Bridge.

Shelford Creek is blocked by a fixed road bridge towards its seaward end and is therefore of little use to yachtsmen, but there is enough water for most small boats to lie afloat in Yokesfleet Creek or the Middleway, which it becomes above the junction of Shelford and New England creeks. About half a mile along the Middleway the channel again divides, this time around Rushley Island. Narrow Cuts, the more easterly arm, is used by craft passing to and from Havengore Bridge. Although it all but dries out at LW, there is enough water in the gutway through Narrow Cuts to allow boats drawing up to 1.5m to get through towards HW. But the narrow channel is tortuous and must be followed, even at HW, to avoid grounding. After leaving Yokesfleet Creek at the junction of the Middleway, keep close to the port hand sea wall up to a sluice, then begin to alter course towards the starboard bank, using the low roof of a distant barn as a mark. There may be a stake marking a hump on the starboard hand and then an even more important red topped stake to be left to port, after which there may be no more marks. On sighting the bridge from Narrow Cuts, do not

be tempted to take a short cut at HW, but remain close to the starboard bank. It is certainly preferable for a stranger – if he can – to make his first acquaintance with Narrow Cuts early on a tide, while the mud is still largely uncovered.

Just before reaching the bridge the channel emerging from Narrow Cuts is joined by Havengore Creek which winds round the western side of Rushey Island to join the Middleway. When bound inwards, there is little point in taking the longer route to the Crouch via Havengore Creek.

The saltings at the southernmost tip of Potton Island extend about 100 metres from the seawall, and are covered at high water springs. The best water runs round this point, about 30 metres from the edge of the saltings; the channel begins to fill at about half tide. When leaving the yard at Wakering, bound for the Roach or Crouch via the Yokesfleet, careful sounding will be necessary as edge of the saltings is unmarked and the leading marks on Rushley Island have gone.

When bound seaward through Havengore Bridge, keep close to the Rushley Island side for about half a mile because best water will not be found on the outside of the bend as might be expected. In recent years a mud bank has extended off Mill Bay at the junction of Potton and Havengore Creeks, deeper draught boats bound for the Havengore Bridge from Potton Creek may need to use the Narrow Cuts route.

Potton Creek

Potton Creek joins the Roach between Potton Island and Barling Ness and runs in a southerly direction to join up with Havengore Creek.

A very long spit extends NE'ly from Barling Ness and it is safest to hold the E shore when entering Barling Creek from the Roach. the first reach in the creek, known locally as 'The Violet', is largely occupied these days by local fishing boats and so it may be difficult to find a space in which to use an anchor.

Barlinghall Creek, leading to Little Wakering Creek, leaves Potton Creek about half a mile south of Barling Ness, and leads up to the villages of Barling and Little Wakering. Although barges used to visit the quays dotted about the upper reaches of these creeks, the landings are mostly disused, and of course no water remains at low tide.

About a quarter of a mile above the junction of Barlinghall Creek, beware of a concrete ford between Potton Island and the mainland. It is not safe to try to pass this way before half-flood. From here, the bridge over Potton Creek will be seen about half a mile ahead. This swing-bridge, which is used only by the Ministry of Defence, will be opened on request –

The MOD swing bridge over Potton Creek will be opened on request during daylight hours

Looking to the north-west from above Havengore Creek, with the bridge in the foreground. Beyond that the creek divides round Rushley Island into the Middleway and Narrow Cuts

VHF Ch 16, 72 ; telephone (01702) 383200; or three toots on a horn, Dutch fashion – at any time during daylight hours two hours either side HW. Keep well over to the E side of the creek when approaching the bridge.

There is a boatyard with a slipway just S of the bridge.

The Havengore Route

This passage to the River Roach across the Maplin Sands and via the Havengore bridge, Narrow Cuts, Middleway and Yokesfleet Creeks should only be made during spring tides, and then only by craft drawing no more than 1.5m.

The approach to Havengore Creek over the Maplins crosses the Shoeburyness Gunnery Range, and as firing is more or less continuous on weekdays, it is as well for yachtsmen to understand their rights and responsibilities when intending to use the Havengore route. The complete bye-laws governing firing practice over the Maplin and Foulness sands are to be found in Statutory Rules and Orders No 714 of 1936, obtainable from HMSO. But the section of these bye-laws which is of greatest importance to yachtsmen reads: *'Any vessel wishing to enter Havengore Creek during such time or times as the whole of the target area is not closed in accordance with Bye-law No 3 must enter the target area not later than half an hour before high water and proceed by the shortest possible course to the Creek.'*

Red flags are hoisted from a number of points along the sea wall; among them at Wakering Stairs and at Havengore Bridge, an hour before firing commences and throughout the period of firing. It is, however, difficult if not impossible to see these signals before setting course across the Maplins from the West Swin.

As firings are almost continuous in daylight hours on weekdays, it is dangerous to make the passage without first obtaining permission. Yachtsmen should telephone the Range Planning Officer at Shoeburyness (see page 67 for details) when, if possible, the bridge will be lifted and firing suspended. Every consideration is given to yachtsmen in this respect.

Night firing is normally confined to periods when the Maplins are uncovered, and in any case, as the swing bridge is no longer manned between sunset and sunrise, the passage cannot be made after dark.

The Maplin sands cannot be crossed from the Swin much earlier than three-quarters flood, and it is impossible for any other than light draught boats to get over the Broomway much before high water. The Broomway was originally a causeway built over the Maplin Sands to connect Foulness Island, and also Havengore and New England Islands, with the mainland at Wakering before any bridge was constructed.

The Broomway stands proud of the mud and sand and there is probably about 1.5 to 2.0m of water over it at HWOS, but often 0.5m or less at HW neaps.

Havengore Creek cannot be distinguished from the West Swin, as any marks off the entrance are too small to be seen over the 2½ miles.

Port Guide: Wakering	
Water	At yard
Stores	None nearer than Gt Wakering (about 1¼ miles)
Repairs	At yard. Slip and cranes
Transport	Buses from Wakering to Southend
Telephone	At yard
Clubs	Wakering Yacht Club
VHF	Ch 68

The survey platform that used to be near the E. Shoebury beacon has been dismantled, but a course of 345°M from the beacon will lead towards the entrance to Havengore Creek. There have been attempts in recent years to establish marks that would assist yachtsmen using the Havengore route but it is extremely difficult to erect structures strong enough to withstand wind and tide for more than a year or so. Two stayed, metal posts were established in 1995: one 200 yards to seaward of the Broomway and one on of the Broomway itself; just west of the first post is a wreck marked with two round markers. The best water is close to these two posts, but although they can be seen easily from the mouth of Havengore Creek they are difficult to make out from seaward against the coastline. There are many other posts and range markers on the sands.

The gutway leading into the creek is no longer buoyed, but once between the sea walls best water will be found towards the N bank up to the bridge.

It must be realised that depths over the Maplins and the Broomway will vary considerably with the direction and strength of wind as well as with barometric pressure. Northerly winds will raise and southerly winds will lower the tidal levels, while a decrease or increase in barometric pressure equivalent to one inch of mercury will respectively raise or lower the depth of water by one foot. Therefore, the more settled the weather, the more likely is the pressure to be high and the tides lower than predicted.

Havengore Bridge

The new bridge over Havengore Creek was opened in November 1988, and its lifting bascule allows unrestricted passage for any yacht. The bridge will be opened as required for 2 hours each side of HW during daylight hours – provided the firing range is not being used. Fortunately, firing seldom takes place at weekends, but anyone planning to use the Havengore route is advised to check by telephoning the Range Operations Officer on Southend (01702) 292271 Ext 3211; or by VHF using the call sign 'SHOE BASE'. The bridge keeper can be contacted during HW periods on VHF (SHOE BRIDGE) or by phone on (01702) 292271 Ext 3436.

The tidal streams hereabouts are somewhat complicated – largely because of the barrier formed by the Broomway. The flood tide from the Roach and the flood over the Maplins meet and cover the Maplins about two hours before HW, after which the tide runs back into Havengore Creek until HW. Then with virtually no period of slack, the ebb runs out of the creek with great strength until the Broomway is again uncovered. These facts should be remembered when using the Havengore route since, when coming from the Swin, it is important to reach the bridge before the ebb commences; and when bound out of the creek it is equally desirable to be at the bridge before the last hour or so of the flood which runs N into Narrow Cuts.

When bound through the bridge and out of the creek it helps the bridge keeper if some kind of signal can be made to indicate that the bridge should be raised. Traffic signals will indicate when it is safe to proceed.

In Conrad's novel Chance, the character Powell was in the habit of disappearing mysteriously from the Thames Estuary in his small cutter, but was eventually followed (probably into Havengore) by Marlow, who describes the chase: '*One afternoon, I made Powell's boat out, heading into the shore. By the time I got close to the mud flats his craft had disappeared inland. But I could see the mouth of the creek by then. The tide being on the turn I took the risk of getting stuck in the mud suddenly and headed in. Before I had gone half a mile, I was up with a building I had seen from the river… it looked like a small barn.*'

There would have been no bridge over the creek when Conrad wrote Chance, but the barn may still exist for a similar building (at Oxenham Farm) can still be seen over the sea walls in the Havengore area.

Looking inland from the Havengore Bridge at near low water. Narrow Cuts curves away to the right, while Havengore Creek bears left, leading to Wakering

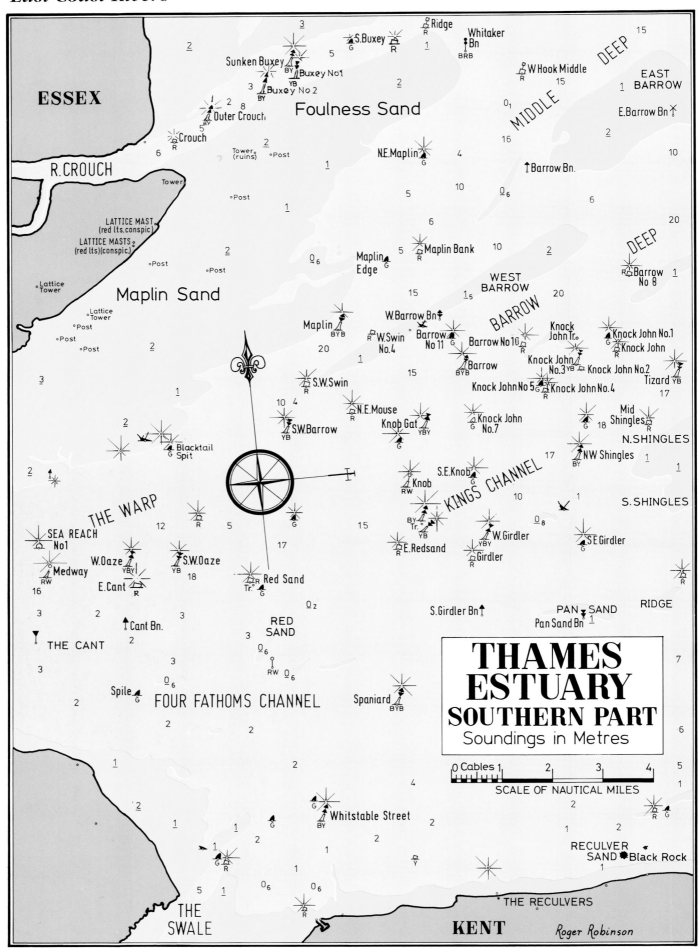

ESSEX

R. CROUCH

Tower

LATTICE MAST
(red lts. conspic.)

LATTICE MASTS
(red lts)(conspic.)

Lattice
Tower

Lattice
Tower

Maplin Sand

°Post

°Post

°Post

Sunken Buxey

Outer Crouch

Crouch

Tower
(ruins) °Post

°Post

S. Buxey Ridge

Buxey No1

Buxey No 2

Foulness Sand

N.E. Maplin

Whitaker
Bn

W Hook Middle

MIDDLE DEEP

EAST
BARROW

E. Barrow Bn

Barrow Bn.

Maplin
Edge

Maplin Bank

WEST
BARROW

DEEP

Barrow
No 8

Maplin

W. Swin
No. 4

Barrow
No 11

W. Barrow Bn

Barrow No 10

BARROW

Knock
John Tr.

Knock John No.1

Knock John

S.W. Swin

Barrow

Knock John
No. 3

Knock John No. 2

Tizard

N.E. Mouse

Knock John No 5 Knock John No. 4

17

S.W. Barrow

Knob Gat

Knock John
No. 7

Mid
Shingles

18

N. SHINGLES

Blacktail
Spit

Knob

S.E. Knob

NW Shingles

KINGS CHANNEL

S. SHINGLES

THE WARP

SEA REACH
No 1

W. Oaze

Medway

E. Cant

S.W. Oaze

Red Sand

E. Redsand

W. Girdler

Girdler

SE Girdler

S. Girdler Bn

PAN SAND

Pan Sand Bn

RIDGE

Cant Bn.

THE CANT

RED
SAND

Spile

FOUR FATHOMS CHANNEL

Spaniard

**THAMES
ESTUARY
SOUTHERN PART**
Soundings in Metres

0 Cables 1   2   3   4

SCALE OF NAUTICAL MILES

Whitstable Street

RECULVER
SAND Black Rock

THE
SWALE

THE RECULVERS

KENT *Roger Robinson*

13. The River Thames

Tides (Southend Pier): HW Dover + 1.20 Range: Springs 5.2m Neaps 3.4m (HW Tower Bridge approx 1.20 after HW Southend)
Charts: Admiralty 1185 (Sea Reach), 2484 (London to Thames Haven), Stanford No 8, Imray C2
Waypoints: NE Maplin Buoy 51.37.43N 01.04.90E Maplin Buoy 51.34.00N 01.02.40E
Blacktail Spit Buoy 51.31.45N 00.56.85E Southend Pierhead 51.30.84N 00.43.51E
Sea Reach No 1 Buoy 51.29.42N 00.52.67E
Hazards: Large ships (steer clear of dredged channel) Floating debris in upper reaches

John Evelyn, whose diary is not so often quoted as that of Samuel Pepys, reported on a day on the Thames he had with Charles II in 1661: *'I sailed this morning with His Majesty in one of his pleasure-boats, vessels not known among us till the Dutch East India Company presented that curious piece to the King: being very excellent sailing vessels. It was a wager between his other new pleasure-boat frigate-like, and one of the Duke of York's – the wager 100-1: the race from Greenwich to Gravesend and back. the King lost in going, the wind being contrary, but saved stakes in returning.'*

Since then there has never been a time when yachts have not sailed on the Thames, and an increasing number of people are visiting London in their boats now that the river is clean and, in the upper reaches, relatively free from commercial traffic. Unfortunately, there are still very few comfortable or attractive anchorages between Leigh and any of the four marinas in or near London, so that a journey up or down the river is best done on one tide when possible.

Before embarking for the first time on a voyage up the London River to Tower Bridge, there are several things to be considered:

1 By using the tide wisely, the distance (some 40 miles) can usually be covered in seven hours, arriving in London just before high water.
2 Do not expect to find any easy or undisturbed anchorages en route.
3 In the upper reaches, keep a particularly keen look-out for floating rafts of debris. Besides drums, crates and bottles these will often include large, half-submerged baulks of timber which can stall an engine, damage a prop or bend a shaft. A particular danger nowadays are invisible plastic sheets.
4 Stow all loose gear. With a fresh wind some reaches of the Thames can be remarkably rough and the wash from fast moving tugs can sometimes come as a surprise.
5 Make sure you understand the procedure for passing through the Thames Barrier in Woolwich Reach.

When sailing in the Thames Estuary or further up-river, it should always be remembered that the dredged channel for shipping is not wide enough to allow a deep-draught vessel to alter course, and in any case there is plenty of water either side of the channel for yachts.

Port Control London can be contacted at Gravesend on VHF Channel 68 for the river above Sea Reach no 4 buoy to Crayfordness, above Crayfordness on Ch 14, and on Channel 12 for the estuary below Sea Reach no 4 buoy. The half-hourly VHF broadcasts are sometimes of interest to yachts, for example, the tide gauge reports.

Approaches

Coming into the Thames from the Channel or the North Sea, it is convenient to consider Sea Reach No 1 buoy as marking the seaward limit of the river. At this point the estuary is about 8 miles wide, to the north Shoeburyness and the Maplin Sands, and to the south, Warden Point and the Isle of Sheppey. The edge of the Maplins is steep-to, but the water shoals more gradually to the south, over an area known as the Cant.

Sea Reach

From Sea Reach No 1 Buoy to Lower Hope Point, some 15 miles up-river, the general direction of the channel is westerly. As there is no really high ground on the Kent shore west of the Medway, a fresh southwesterly wind blowing against the flood tide will kick up a short steep sea.

Shipping bound up the Thames follows the well marked Yantlet dredged channel, which has a least depth of 10m and a width of about 2 cables up as far as Shell Haven. This channel is marked by a series of seven 'Special' buoys, either pillar or spherical, and coloured either yellow or with red and white vertical stripes. But small craft will normally prefer to steer clear of the main channel, and fortunately there is plenty of water on both sides.

When following an inward course to the north of the dredged channel, a watch must be kept for an obstruction to navigation extending off-shore to a point about 1 mile SE of Shoeburyness. This obstruction – part of a wartime barrier/boom – has a light (Fl Y 2.5s) but does not reach as far as the drying edge of Maplin Sands, although another post (Fl (3) G 10s) does mark the point where the barrier once reached deep water.

If visibility is reasonable, Southend Pier can be seen from abreast the Shoeburyness obstruction, although a direct course between the two is not advisable between half-ebb and half-flood because it leads over the edge of drying flats. Instead, the West Shoeburyness (Con G Fl G 2.5s) should be left to starboard or close to port.

There is a Coastguard and radio direction finding station at Shoeburyness.

Southend Pier

This mile-long pier dates from 1829 and seems never to be out of trouble for very long. A fire at the pierhead in 1978 destroyed the Coastguard and Lloyd's stations, a freighter cut clean through the structure and wrecked the RNLI station in 1986, and in 1995 the bowling alley at the landward end was destroyed by fire. Much of the damage has been repaired and the pier is up and running again. It is even possible for a yacht to tie up alongside for a while to take on water or collect stores from the town. The local RNLI station is at the head of the pier.

For a mile or more on either side of the pier, there are some 3,000 small boat moorings – all of them drying out on to a more or less muddy bottom.

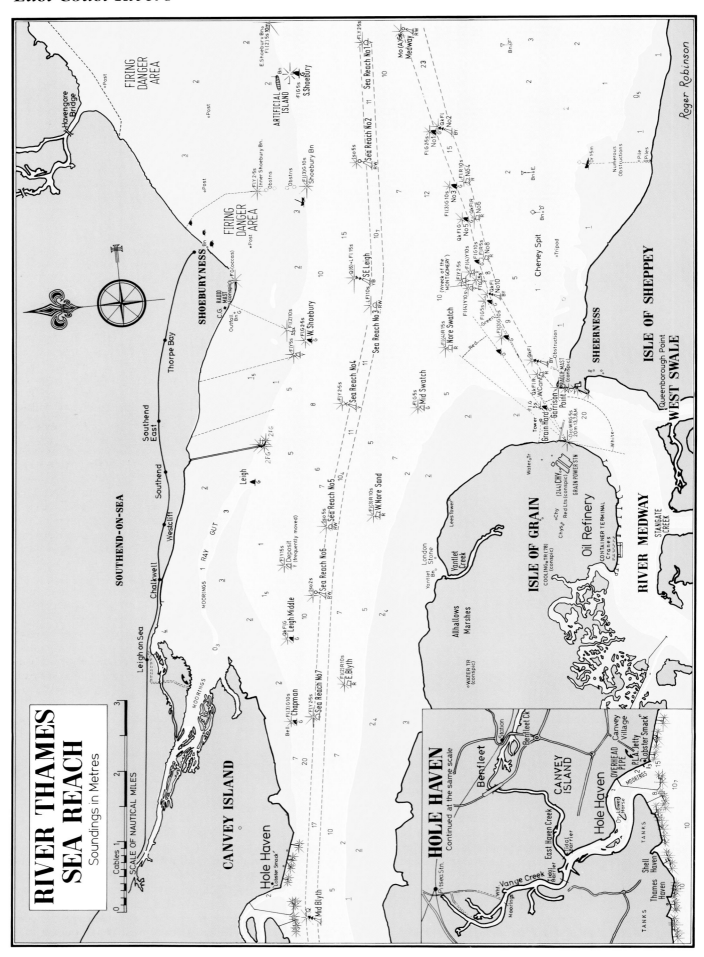

Diagonally from the bottom right can be seen Theobald's Wharf alongside the Strand, as well as the cockle sheds and the boatyard beside the railway station at Leigh-on-Sea

There is plenty of water off the end of the pier (5m or 6m) and an anchorage can usually be found on the edge of the flats on either side. There is little protection except from the north.

During the sailing season there are spherical red racing buoys on the N side of the Sea Reach Channel off Southend.

From the end of Southend Pier, a course due west (M) will lead to the West Leigh Middle buoy (Con G Q G). Leigh Middle is a shoal area that almost dries out along the S edge of the drying sands that extend eastward from Canvey Point.

A spoil ground buoy is usually located somewhere to the E of W Leigh Middle buoy, and is often in little more than 2m at LWS. The westerly course continued past the W Leigh Middle buoy will lead about a quarter of a mile south of the drying edge of the Chapman Sands half a mile off the Canvey Island shore. A green conical bell buoy (Fl (3) G 10s) is established close south of the old lighthouse position. The edge of the sand near here is steep-to, there being depths of 20m within half a cable of the light.

A westerly (Mag) course held for another 1½ miles will pass close to Scars Elbow (no longer marked by a buoy) at the E end of a series of jetties with a background of oil containers on shore.

At certain states of tide – particularly during the ebb at springs, considerable overfalls occur about 300m S of Scars Elbow, where there is a patch of hard, broken ground. Because of this, it will often pay to pass farther south, near the dredged channel, which hereabouts is only half a mile from the north shore.

About a mile west of Scars Elbow is the entrance to Holehaven Creek – a favourite anchorage with earlier generations of Thames yachtsmen, but becoming less attractive as each year passes and our appetite for oil increases. At one time there was a half-mile gap between the tanker jetties, making the position of Holehaven obvious, but another jetty has been erected directly opposite Hole Haven Bay so that the opening is less easy to distinguish.

There are no further marks on the north side of Sea Reach, but there is deep water right up to the numerous jetties, dolphins and mooring buoys that serve the oil refineries and storage depots. All the jetties and dolphins show two vertical fixed green lights at night.

Powerful traffic lights are shown up and down the river from Holehaven Point and Scars Elbow when tankers are berthing or unberthing.

Leigh-on-Sea

Almost the whole of the foreshore of the adjoining towns of Leigh, Westcliff and Southend dries out soon after half-ebb, so yachts drawing more than 1m should not expect to cross Canvey Point Shoals or Marsh End sands at less than three hours before or after high water.

Leigh Creek, however, does enable craft of moderate draught to reach the quays at Old Leigh, and the town is interesting and important to yachtsmen because of its several boat yards.

Except at or near to HW, an approach to Leigh should be made from a position close to the Leigh or 'Low-Way' buoy (Con G), located about half a mile W of Southend Pier. Although the Leigh buoy is conical and green it must be considered a port-hand mark when entering the Ray Gut. A recent amateur survey carried out by members of the Leigh SC showed that there is practically no water to the W of it at LWS.

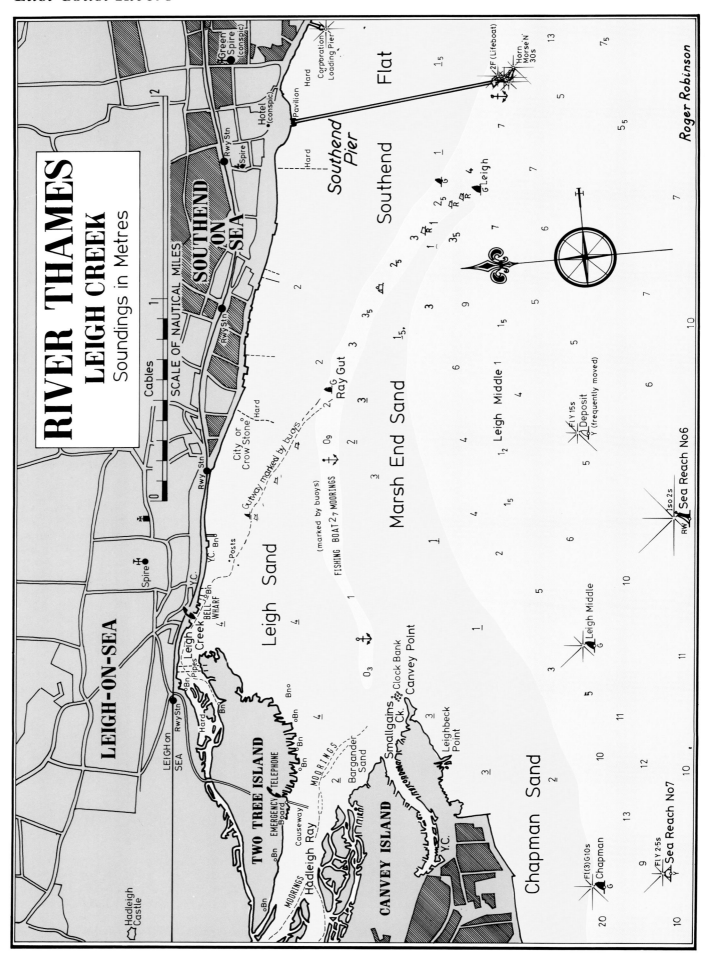

RIVER THAMES
LEIGH CREEK
Soundings in Metres

Roger Robinson

Port Guide: Leigh-on-Sea

Water	From Bell Wharf or Yacht Club
Stores	From shops in town nearby. EC Wed
Chandler	Near Bell Wharf
Repairs	Several boatyards with slips or cranes and travel hoist
Fuel	Diesel from yard
Transport	Good train service to London (Fenchurch Street)
Telephone	Outside The Smack
Clubs	Leigh-on-Sea Sailing Club. Essex Yacht Club. Alexandra Yacht Club (Southend). Thames Estuary Yacht Club (Westcliff). Thorpe Bay Yacht Club

Approaching Benfleet Yacht Club early on the tide

The Gut is just over a cable wide between its steep-to banks, and it carries some 3 metres at LW for a distance of nearly a mile in a generally north-westerly direction. A little way in from the entrance, deep water in the Ray is indicated by permanent moorings and fishing craft.

The channel leading to Leigh Creek and the Creek itself have been re-marked recently as the result of cooperation between Southend Council and local fishermen. But unless a craft is able to take the ground without much inconvenience, it will be preferable to bring up in Hadleigh Ray, where several of the local bawleys are usually moored. There is enough water to stay afloat in Hadleigh Ray almost as far west as Canvey Point, but there is little protection except from the north.

At or near HW, a cross-sand route may be taken direct from West Leigh Middle Buoy to Bell Wharf on a bearing of 005°M.

It is sometimes possible for a deeper draught boat to find a berth alongside Bell Wharf, where Leigh Creek closely approaches the old town of Leigh. There is a landing place – a narrow strip of beach – just west of Bell Wharf, and it is also possible towards HW to land on the groynes farther E, close to the clubship Bembridge belonging to the Essex YC.

From Leigh it is about two miles to Hadleigh Castle from which there are striking views of the estuary just as there were in Constable's day.

Hadleigh Ray and Benfleet Creek

The deep water moorings in Hadleigh Ray extend westward almost to Canvey Point, but thereafter only the shallowest of craft can remain afloat throughout even a neap tide. However, there are hundreds of small craft moored between Canvey Point and the causeway at Two-Tree Island and in Smallgains Creek, the entrance to which is marked by an E cardinal buoy abreast Canvey Point. The landing and launching place on Two-Tree island is approached from the Ray via a shoal patch, which may easily stop a yacht around low water. Otherwise, a course from one moored yacht to the next, following the larger craft, will lead to the causeway, which extends to the low water mark.

There is a car park and a road to Leigh Station. A

Port Guide: Benfleet

Water	From yacht club or yard
Stores	Shops in Benfleet
Repairs	Shipwright near bridge; slipway
Fuel	Petrol and diesel
Transport	Trains to London (Fenchurch Street)
Club	Benfleet Yacht Club (Tel: 01268 792278)

hard-master is present during the day and there is water available while he is there, together with an emergency telephone.

Benfleet Bridge is about two miles from the causeway at Two-Tree Island, and the channel of the creek is best learned by sailing up early on the tide. The gutway is marked by a series of numbered red port-hand buoys, and two or three green starboard-hand marks. There is a beacon with a conical topmark on the north shore near No 5 buoy, and at this point course must be changed to bring a pair of leading marks in line on the opposite (S) bank. The front one of these two beacons has a triangle topmark and the other a diamond shaped topmark. Moorings are then continuous up to Benfleet Bridge, and these indicate the channel.

Benfleet YC produces a chart of Benfleet Creek, copies of which can be obtained by visiting yachtsmen, who are welcome at the fine clubhouse, alongside one of the best slipways in the Thames Estuary.

Smallgains Creek

This little creek off the eastern tip of Canvey Island is hardly more than a mile long, but is packed with moorings and stagings belonging to the Island YC, whose clubhouse is near the head of the creek.

Port Guide: Canvey Island (eastern end)

Water	At Club
Stores	All kinds
Repairs	Yards at the Point. Dry dock
Transport	From Benfleet Station (2 miles)
Clubs	Island Yacht Club. Chapman Sands SC

The Kent Shore

If the course in from the Estuary has been along the Kent coast, S of the dredged channel and N of the Medway channel, then a course keeping about half a mile S of the Yantlet dredged channel, will serve as far as the East Blyth buoy, some five miles away.

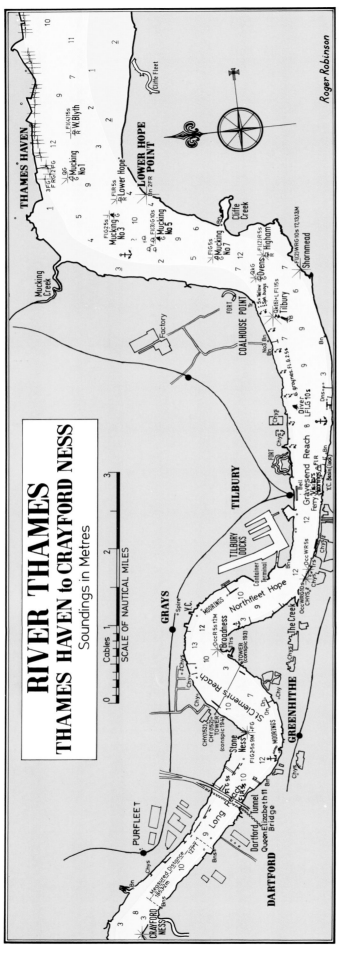

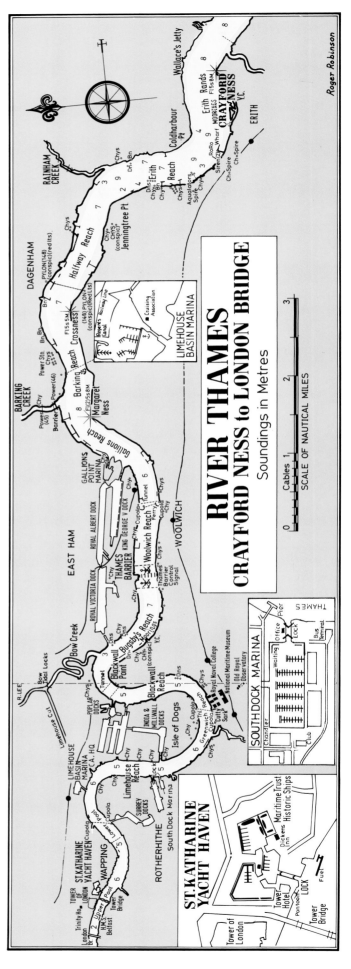

Edward Clack

Most boats are moored to stagings or pontoons at the head of Benfleet Creek, where the Benfleet Yacht Club has its clubhouse and slipway

The Nore Sand (the first shoal ever to be marked with a light in the Thames Estuary in 1732) used to dry out, but now has nowhere less than a fathom (2m) over it.

When passing south of the Nore Sand, as from the Medway, an entrance to the swathway should be shaped from a position close to the Nore Swatch buoy (Can R Fl(4)R 15s). From this mark, a course approximately 300°M will lead close to the Mid Swatch buoy (Con G Fl G 5s) guarding the south side of the shoal. Close south of the Mid Swatch buoy there is 8-9 metres, but there is little more than two cables between the buoy and the very steep edge of Grain sands to the S. The same course (300°M) continued from the Mid Swatch buoy will lead out of the swathway and up to the W Nore Sand (Can R Fl(3)R 10s).

Yantlet Creek

There are not many landmarks along the south shore of Sea Reach, but the Yantlet Beacon (black with ball topmark) marking the west side of the entrance to Yantlet Creek can be seen from the W Nore Sand buoy. Small craft can reach this creek via a gutway running roughly north-easterly through the Yantlet Flats, and there is a 'hole' carrying about a metre, approximately a cable SW of the beacon.

The place is still used by yachtsmen in search of a remote and secluded anchorage although the whole area is close to by the remains of the great oil refinery located just to the south on the Isle of Grain. However, a useful temporary anchorage can be found along the edge of Yantlet Flats in about 4m.

The next light buoy is the E Blyth (Can R Fl(2)R 10s), located about a quarter of a mile off the edge of the flats, which at this point extend for almost a mile from the Kent shore. The drying edge is particularly steep-to abreast the

E Blyth buoy although it shelves more gradually farther west, and changes from sand to sand and mud and then mud alone at the western end of the Sea Reach. The next buoy is the Mid Blyth – particularly useful to yachtsmen coming down river, as it is a convenient mark from which to set a course to the entrance of Holehaven.

Holehaven

Holehaven beacon is not easy to distinguish on the east side of the entrance to the creek but it bears approximately 50° M from the Mid Blyth buoy, and is about half a mile distant. At HW, the entrance to Holehaven appears easy because of its apparent width, but in fact the only deep water runs about half a cable from the Canvey, or east side of the inlet. Drying mud with a steep-to edge stretches for nearly half a mile from Shellhaven Point. After entering, a useful leading line is usually provided by the craft already moored or anchored in the creek, all of which should be left close to port.

There is only about 1.5m of water in the entrance abreast the beacon at LWS, but once over this bar depths increase to more than 2m past the PLA pier while, about a quarter of a

Port Guide: Holehaven	
Pier Master	Phone: Canvey 01268 683041 or 0836 248472.*
Water	From yard of Lobster Smack (by request), or at PLA jetty
Stores, petrol, oil etc	From Canvey village (1 mile). EC Thurs
Transport	Buses from Canvey village to South Benfleet. Trains from S Benfleet to London

Graham Jones

A smack off Coalhouse Point, with the chimneys at Tilbury in the background

Port Guide: Gravesend	
Canal Basin	
Lock-keeper	Tel: 01474 352392
Water	From standpipe near entrance to lock
Stores	From shops in town. EC Wed
Chandler	Nearby
Fuel	Petrol from garage in Milton Road
Crane	Inside the basin, can be used with permission from club
Club	Gravesend SC (formed in 1884) Tel: 01474 533974

mile inside, soundings increase to more than 5m in a 'hole' which no doubt gave the creek its name. Although the best water in this first reach is well over towards the east bank, it is necessary to choose an anchorage carefully on the edge of the mud on the west side of the channel, because the Canvey Island shore is embanked with stone and has stone groynes extending well into the deeper water. Furthermore, towards HW, at night as well as in the daytime, there is regular lighter traffic through the creek, the lighters being towed in strings which swing wide behind their tug.

Fortunately the holding is good near the edge of the mud along the west side of the channel, but there is some risk of swinging on to the mud unless a kedge is used. Riding lights are essential at night. Both flood and ebb tides run at about 2½ knots at springs and are strongest near the Canvey shore.

Landing, to consult the piermaster, is permitted at the PLA jetty, but otherwise there is a wooden causeway just to the south of the pier. Once over the sea wall, the Lobster Smack will be there waiting for you as it has for generations of sailing men before.

About half a mile within the entrance an overhead pipe line crosses the creek from the new jetty to Canvey Island. This structure gives a clearance of 30ft (9.2m) at HWS so some boats can pass under and proceed with the tide towards Pitsea, Vange or Benfleet. At Benfleet there is a fixed bridge with only 6ft (2m) clearance at HWS.

Vange Creek

There are many small boat moorings in this creek, which leads up to the Watt Tyler Country Park, renamed Pitsea Hall (1995), home of the National Motorboat Museum. There is a slipway, a workshop and telephone nearby. Pitsea station is about a mile away.

The London River

Lower Hope

Above Thames Haven, the river turns south round Lower Hope Point into Lower Hope Reach, the width of which diminishes quite quickly from about two miles down to less than a mile off Coalhouse Point. There is room to anchor on Mucking Flats well out of the channel and inside a line of large mooring buoys near to Mucking No 5 buoy (Con G Gp Fl(3)G 10s). This can be a useful place to be in a strong SW'ly. The 'Tilbury' buoy (S Car YB QkFl(6) LFl 15s) off Coalhouse Point is the last of the channel buoys and, for the rest of the way up-river, shore marks are used to navigate from reach to reach.

Gravesend

Gravesend Reach runs for about four miles in an EW direction, with Tilbury Docks to the north and Gravesend to the south of the river. To help scour the Diver shoal, the PLA has built six groynes on the north side of the reach, marked by lit (Fl G) beacons, which are difficult to see coming upriver by day. There are five unlit yellow buoys just downstream of the first groyne off Coalhouse Point and there is no passage inshore of these or the beacons. The best course is from north of the Ovens buoy to Tilbury S Cardinal, and then to leave Diver buoy close to starboard.

On the north shore, the Gravesend ferry and cruise liners use the Tilbury landing stage.

At night piers and stagings of the north bank are marked by two fixed green lights (vert) and those on the south side by vertical pairs of red lights.

The Gravesend Canal Basin bears a large sign – Gravesham Marina. Entry and departure through the lock gates are controlled by traffic lights. The lock-keeper (Tel: 01474 352392) is normally on duty around the time of HW, and the gates can be opened from 1½ hrs before until just after HW.

A temporary mooring can sometimes be found off the Gravesend Sailing Club, where there are two visitors' buoys, one of which can dry out at LWS, but the other, at the east end of the club moorings and marked Visitors, gives a clear depth of 2m at all times. There are steps for landing at the lockside near high water, but at other times, use the PLA slipway opposite the rowing club at the W end of the Promenade, where it is possible to anchor. A convenient anchorage can also be found to the east of the long Clubbs jetty, near the Sea School, but it is difficult to get ashore.

Assistance is always available from members of the Gravesend SC at weekends. The club has scrubbing posts near the river wall and masts can be stepped or unstepped by prior arrangement. Craft should not be left unattended in the Gravesend anchorage, but arrangements can usually be made with the Lock Master to leave a boat in the Canal Basin.

If bound up-river, it is not very useful to emerge from the lock at Gravesend just before HW so it will sometimes be preferable to lie to an anchor in the river throughout an ebb tide. This can be done by choosing a spot about a mile down-river from the lock, just below the Ship and Lobster. The holding ground is good, and there is room to swing well out of the fairway. This is a time honoured anchorage but it is not easy to get ashore and is remote from Gravesend.

Grays Thurrock

Northfleet Hope adjoins Gravesend Reach and runs SE-NW for just over a mile to Broadness on the south bank and Grays Thurrock on the north bank.

Moorings belonging to members of the Thurrock YC (tel: 01375 373720) are located just below the town causeway and abreast the wreck of the old lightship that once served as

The tidal surge barrier at Woolwich

Graham Jones

the club's headquarters. The club now has a new building nearby, where visiting yachtsmen are welcomed and sometimes a mooring can be arranged. All kinds of supplies from the town nearby.

Greenhithe

There are some small boat moorings and a useful causeway at Greenhithe, opposite Stone Ness (Fl 2.5s), and anchorage can usually be found in line with, and to the west, of the Paper Mills jetty.

Queen Elizabeth II Bridge

This impressive bridge between Dartford in Kent and Thurrock in Essex, with its 54 metres vertical clearance, presents no problem to the yachtsman. However, there are Ro-Ro berths on both banks in Long Reach, up and downstream of the bridge.

Erith Rands

This short reach between Crayford Ness and the town of Erith runs for about a mile in an E-W direction.

A useful anchorage can be found on the S shore in Anchor Bay, where the Erith YC (tel: 01322 332943) has its headquarters in the old Norwegian car ferry Folgefonn. The club has moorings abreast the clubship and a buoy can usually be found for a visitor. If anchoring, a berth should be sought either above or below the line of club moorings.

A landing can be made a the club causeway, where there is a standpipe. A telephone at the club is useful for calling a taxi to save walking into Erith for supplies.

Gallions Reach

The new (1997) Gallions Point Marina, entered via a lock at the old entrance to the Albert Dock, provides a useful stopover down river of the Thames Barrier and offers over 100 berths, with more planned. Telephone 0171 4767054 VHF Ch 37 80. Woolwich Ferry and foot tunnel are about 15 minutes walk.

Woolwich Reach

When passing through Woolwich Reach, there are two hazards to contend with – the ferries which ply between north and south Woolwich, and the Thames Barrier about halfway along the reach.

The Thames Barrier

At the tidal-surge barrier across the Thames in Woolwich Reach a system of extremely powerful light signals is used by day and night to indicate which spans are to be used and which are barred to traffic. Two green arrows pointing inwards will be displayed from each side of a span that is open to oncoming traffic, while red crosses shown from each side of a span will mean that no traffic must pass through the span in that direction. Anchoring is prohibited in the vicinity of the barrier.

Large illuminated notice boards are in position upstream near Blackwall Point and downstream near Cross Ness and amber lights shown at these boards warn ships to proceed with caution while red lights require them to stop. Audible warnings can also be issued from these stations.

Port Control London advises yachtsmen to talk to traffic control on VHF Channel 14, call sign Woolwich Radio; or on 0181 855 0315, if without VHF.

Barrier closures

From time to time the Barrier is closed for testing purposes, usually only one gate at any one time but occasionally all gates at the same time. Information regarding the dates and times of closures are given by Woolwich Radio on Ch 14 and in PCL's Notice to Mariners.

Drying moorings of the Greenwich YC (tel: 0181 8587339) are situated on the south side of the river in the bight between Woolwich and Bugsby's reaches. As part of the Tideway Sailing Centre the club now has extensive premises and many new moorings, including some for visitors who must be prepared to dry out if staying for a whole tide. There is a shingle patch near the causeway and this can be useful if a propeller has been fouled by debris in the river. Anchorage is possible on good holding ground on the same side of the river.

Greenwich Reach

This short E-W reach links Blackwall and Limehouse reaches round the Isle of Dogs. The Royal Naval College is prominent on the south bank and near it is the National Maritime Museum, the Cutty Sark and Gipsy Moth IV, while not far away at Deptford, the Mary Rose was built in the first year of the reign of Henry VIII.

Small craft can usually anchor just below and in line with Greenwich Pier, which is much used by water buses and pleasure steamers.

South Dock Marina

Part of the old Surrey Dock complex on the S bank of the river has now been converted into the South Dock Marina. the locked entrance, from Limehouse Reach, about three miles down river from Tower Bridge, will be operated for about

St Katharine Yacht Haven is superbly sited close to the Tower of London and immediately below Tower Bridge – photo courtesy of Taylor Woodrow

two hours either side of HW. There are berths for some 350 craft, with all the usual marina facilities. Tel: 0171 252 2244, VHF Ch M 37 or 80. London City Airport is conveniently near.

Limehouse Basin Marina

On the N bank the former Regents Canal Dock now contains the 90-berth Limehouse Basin Marina, and provides access to the inland waterways network. The Basin also houses the headquarters of the Cruising Association (telephone number 0171-537 2828 VHF Ch 80), managers of the marina on behalf of British Waterways. The CA bar and restaurant are open to all visiting yachtsmen; there are no fuelling facilities The lock operates all week, 0800-1800 April 1st to October 31st and 0800-1600 November 1st to March 31st. There is 1 metre over the sill at LW Neaps, and access is possible one and a half hours either side of LW. Easy travel to London is available via the Docklands Light Railway.

St Katharine Yacht Haven

St Katharine Yacht Haven is close to the Tower of London and immediately below Tower Bridge on the north bank of the river. This busy marina, with berthing facilities for more than 200 craft, must surely be one of the most superbly sited yacht harbours in the world.

Entry to the harbour is by way of a tidal lock (30ft X 100ft) which can be worked for about two hours either side of HW, between 0600 and 2030 in summer and between 0800 and 1800 in winter. There is a permanent harbourmaster, telephone 0171-481 8350; VHF Ch 80.

A 30m pontoon downstream of the entrance to the harbour may be used by craft arriving outside locking times, and nearby is a fuel (diesel) pontoon.

The inside of St Katharine pier can be used by yachtsmen wanting to get ashore while awaiting entry to the marina (the outside is heavily used by ferries and trip boats).

The entrance to Limehouse Basin Marina, which houses the headquarters of the Cruising Association, and also gives access to the Inland Waterways system

14. The Medway

Tides (Queenborough): HW Dover + 1.35 Range: Springs 5.1m Neaps 3.3m
Charts: Admiralty 1834 (Grain Pt to folly Pt), 1835 (Folly Pt to Rochester), Stanford No 5, Imray Y18
Waypoints: Medway Lt Buoy 51.28.80N 00.52.92E S Montgomery Buoy 51.27.88N 00.47.17E
Grain Hard Buoy 51.26.94N 00.44.27E Queenborough Spit Buoy 51.25.78N 00.44.03E
Hazards: Wreck of the Richard Montgomery. Overfalls near Sheerness Fort on ebb

For centuries, the Medway was the Navy's river, with dockyard bases at Sheerness and Chatham, and the even older forts at Folly Point and Darnett Ness. The first warship built at Chatham was launched in 1586, and at the Historic Dockyard and Museum you can see the most complete Georgian/early Victorian dockyard in the world.

For the yachtsman, the Medway offers very good sailing in the lower reaches where on the south side there are some quiet anchorages in settings that can have changed little since the Romans established their potteries and even less since the prison-hulks were moored in the area during the Revolutionary and Napoleonic wars. Those who are not afraid of mud can still find relics of both these periods, even though they were separated by thousands of years. By contrast, the north shore of the river as far west as Long Reach is now almost entirely given over to an oil refinery, a power station and a container terminal.

The river is navigable by quite large vessels for some 13 miles from its mouth at Sheerness to Rochester, where the headroom under the bridge is 30ft at LWS. The tide flows for a further 12 miles to Allington Lock, one mile above the lower arched bridge at Aylsford. Then, for a further 17 miles, the river winds through pleasant country to Maidstone and Tonbridge, with eleven locks. Craft drawing 2m can reach Maidstone, while those drawing 1.2m can reach Tonbridge. Maximum length 18m, beam 4.5m.

Since 1968, the Medway Port Authority (now the Port of Sheerness) has been responsible for the ports at Sheerness, Isle of Grain, Faversham and Rochester. There is a considerable commercial traffic in both the Medway and the Swale.

Medway Ports VHF Ch 74 and 16 Medway Radio Harbourmaster Tel: 01795 561234

Landmarks

From the Thames Estuary the tree-covered cliffs of Warden Point on the Isle of Sheppey, some six miles east of the entrance, are conspicuous. On the west are the tall chimneys of the oil refinery and the new Grain Power Station, the chimney of the latter being 800ft high and therefore the most prominent daylight mark in the whole of the Thames Estuary, sometimes visible from as far north as the Wallet. The chimney displays four sets of four vertical red lights, the top ones of which are flashing.

On the east side of the entrance there is the fort at Garrison

The wreck of the ammunition ship Richard Montgomery lies beside the dredged channel into the Medway, but it is guarded on all sides by yellow buoys

Edward Clack

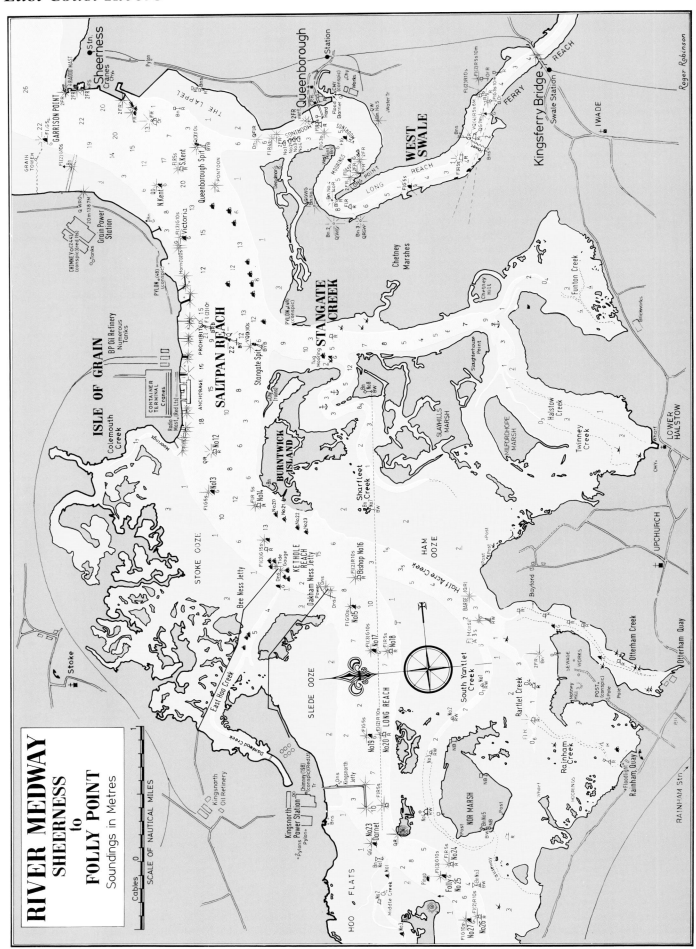

Frazer Cork

When you use the impressive all-tide landing pontoon at Queenborough, remember you will need to obtain a token to get back on it

Point, Sheerness, from which a powerful flashing light is shown by day or night when large tankers are under way, while on the west side the massive buildings of the power station are very prominent.

Approaches

There are three main approaches to the Medway (see page 70): (i) The main deep water route. From the Medway Pillar Lt Buoy (R W V S Iso 2s Sph topmark) some three-quarters of a mile south of Sea Reach No 1 Buoy, the channel runs in a W by S'ly direction between Sheerness Middle Sand and Grain Spit to the west, and the flats of the Cant to the east. It is wide and well lit, all the starboard hand buoys having white or green lights and the port having red. The stranded wreck of the ammunition ship Richard Montgomery lies on Sheerness Middle Sand, very near No 7 and No 9 buoys. It is dangerous but very well marked by special buoys (yellow) on all sides. The tidal stream off the approach sets W by N and E by S at a max rate of 2½ and 3 knots respectively, slightly across the channel, but as Garrison Point is neared they run fairly up and down the channel.

(ii) The Nore Swatch, formerly known as the Jenkin Swatch, is not quite so important now that the Nore Sand has 2m or more over it at LWS. From the west the Swatch can be located by the West Nore Sand Lt Buoy (Can R Fl(3) R 10s) which lies on the south side of Sea Reach almost opposite Southend Pier. A course of 120°M leads to pass the Mid Swatch light buoy (Con G Fl G 5s) close to port and, continued, reaches the Nore Swatch light buoy (Can r Fl(4)R 15s). From here a S'ly course leaving Grain Edge Buoy (Con G) to starboard leads into the main channel.

(iii) Across the Cant. Vessels making from the eastward via the 'Four Fathom Channel' or out of the West Swale, can carry about 3m least water on a course 300°M from the Spile Buoy (Con G Fl G 2.5s), keeping about two miles from the Sheppey shore. Several unlit beacons and Cheney Spit, a shingle bank with about 1m least water, extend eastwards from Garrison Point. These hazards make it inadvisable to get much closer than a mile offshore. Cheney Rocks, an unmarked drying patch of stones, lies half a mile off the eastern end of Sheerness town. A N cardinal buoy (QFl) marks the seaward end of an obstruction extending from the shore just east of Garrison Point. Tides over the Cant are slacker than those in the channels. The Medway may also be entered through the Swale (see Chapter 15).

Entrance

The entrance to the Medway is between Garrison Point to port and Grain Hard buoy (Con G Fl G 5s) to starboard.

Massive landmarks have been created on the west side of the entrance in the form of Grain Power Station with its enormous buildings and 800ft chimney, the latter showing four vertical red lights at night.

Garrison Point is steep-to, but small craft working close inshore from the east should be careful to avoid the sewer outfall just outside it, the end of which is marked by a N Cardinal Pillar buoy (BY Q). On the first of the ebb during spring tides, there are considerable overfalls on the east side of the entrance near the Garrison shore.

A powerful white light (Fl 7s) shown from Garrison Point means that a large tanker is under way, and small craft must keep clear.

On the Grain shore the flats run out for half a mile almost to the Grain Hard buoy. No attempt should be made to pass to the west of this buoy as there are the remains of an obstruction running out from the Martello Tower.

Once inside, the river broadens out, and the former Sheerness Naval Dockyard, now a busy commercial harbour, will be seen to port. The flood runs at 2½ knots at springs, setting sharply on to Garrison Point, and causing a pronounced north-going eddy along the Sheppey shore.

The ebb runs hard, 3 knots or more at springs on the Sheerness side causing overfalls, but is much weaker on the Grain side of the river, so a yacht entering against the stream should seek this shore, remembering that the edge of the mud is quite steep.

Anchoring is prohibited on the NW side of the river because of the commercial traffic. On the east shore The Lappel, is no longer a suitable anchorage, as it has been largely infilled for a container/car park which is often brilliantly illuminated at night.

Queenborough

A much better and more sheltered berth will be found at Queenborough, a mile and a half further south and just inside the West Swale. The entrance is narrow and is marked by Queenborough Spit Pillar buoy (E Car BYB Q(3) (10s) which should be left close to starboard. After this, two dolphins with flashing red lights, marking the remains of the old packet pier, should be left strictly to port because of the extremely foul ground inside them. The Queenborough pier was in regular

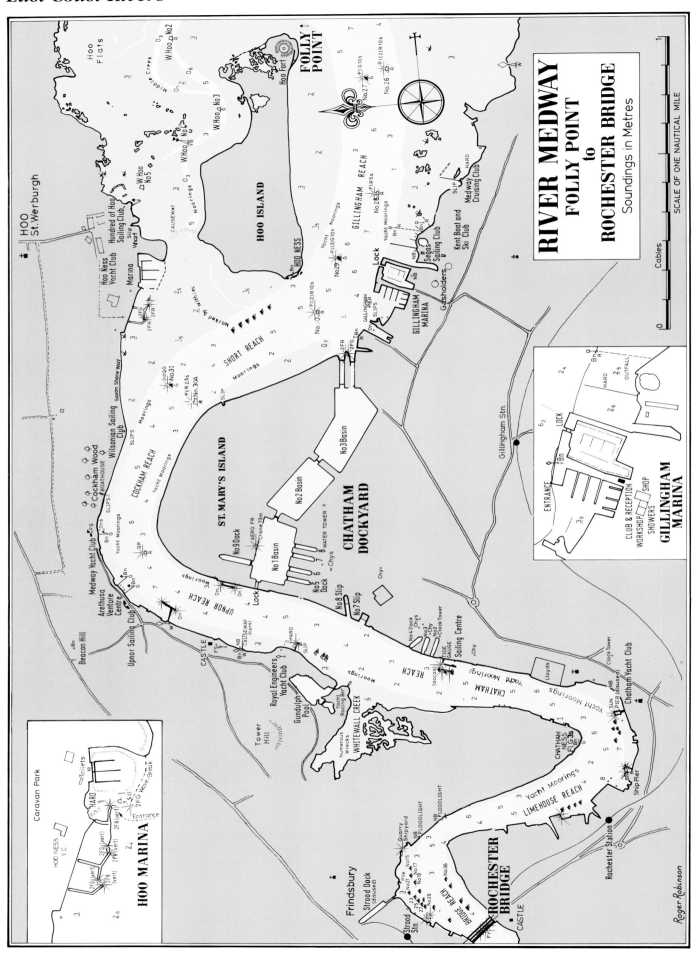

RIVER MEDWAY
FOLLY POINT
to
ROCHESTER BRIDGE
Soundings in Metres

GILLINGHAM MARINA

HOO MARINA

Roger Robinson

Queenborough Yacht Club can be found near the top of the all-tide landing pontoon

use by the Flushing ferry a hundred years ago, but, although there was a brief revival, the Sheerness-Flushing service is no longer.

For the next mile or more the river is lined on both sides by more than a hundred moorings that are controlled by the Swale Borough Council. Four large yellow buoys near the hard are intended for rafting by visitors, up to four boats on each. Trot Boat operates a ferry at weekends which can be

Port Guide: Queenborough	
Supervisor	Harbourmaster on Town Quay (Tel 01795 662051) VHF Channel 74 Call sign SHEPPEY ONE.
Water	On all-tide landing or tap near top of causeway
Stores	Shops in town. EC Wed
Repairs	Yard with slip in Queenborough Creek
Fuel	From yard at head of creek or garages in town
Chandler	Near top of hard
Transport	Train service to London via Chatham. Station ½ mile
Water Taxi	call Queen Base Cc M80, M2
Clubs	Sheppey YC (Cruiser Section). Queenborough YC (restaurant and bar) Tel: 01795 663955

contacted on VHF. It should be noted that the hard extends a long way and care must be taken to avoid its submerged end.

The local council owns the all-tide landing facility with a T-head floating pontoon, marked by 2 FR vertical lights, just down-river from the hard. This makes getting ashore for stores and water much easier, but remember that to get back onto the pontoon via the gate, you need to purchase a token from the Queenborough Yacht Club, the chandlers, the pub or any town trader. Stay alongside is limited to 15 minutes, unless prior arrangement can be made with the harbourmaster.

There is a concrete barge, used for mooring, on the west side of the river, opposite the causeway. The east side of the channel is marked by a red can (Fl R 3s). Anchorage is forbidden in the fairway because of the large commercial ships that come by, but a berth can usually be found close to the mud on the east side of the river just south of the causeway, although the holding ground is not too good.

Keep clear of the entrance to Queenborough Creek, a narrow gut that leads in behind the town, the course of which is marked by half a dozen red can and green conical buoys. Queenborough Quay can be reached via the creek around HW.

The tide runs south past Queenborough for the first hour after HW.

Sheerness to Rochester

Standing on up the Medway through Saltpan Reach the river widens and tidal streams are less strong. Almost the whole of the north shore is occupied by tanker and container ship berths and these are marked by vertical pairs of fixed green lights. At the western end of all these jetties is Colemouth Creek, which formerly joined the Yantlet Creek in the Thames to form the Isle of Grain. This carries 2m at low water for half a mile, but is of little interest because of its environment.

Very few yachtsmen sailing past the Power Station, Refinery and Container Port on the Isle of Grain, will know that in 1897, the Royal Corinthian Yacht Club made a deal with the South Eastern Railway Company to move their headquarters from Erith to Port Victoria. A splendid clubhouse was erected and members came down from London by train to join their yachts on moorings opposite Stangate Creek.

A line of large, unlit buoys extends along the south side of Saltpan Reach about ½ mile east of the entrance to Stangate Creek. Three other mooring buoys (Nos 2, 3 and 4) are located in mid-channel, the first and last of which are lit (Q R).

Stangate Creek

This creek, running south of Saltpan Reach, provides perhaps the most useful anchorage in the Medway. A spit extends from the western side of Stangate Creek and this is marked by an E Cardinal pillar buoy (BYBVQ (3) 5s). The eastern side of the entrance is fairly steep-to.

Half a mile into the creek wreckage on the starboard hand is marked by a green conical buoy and just beyond, opposite a red can buoy, is the entrance to Sharfleet Creek.

For a further mile to the south, the depths in Stangate Creek decrease gradually from some 10m to about 4m LWS at Slaughterhouse Point, where the creek divides. Funton Creek to port holds water for only a little way, but can provide a quiet berth. To starboard, the main channel carries 2m for a quarter of a mile or so and then divides again into Halstow, Twinney and Milford Hope Creeks, all of which dry out. At tide time it is possible for shoal draught craft to reach the wharf at the head of Halstow Creek, where there is a Saxon church, an inn and the Lower Halstow SC. If staying, on must take the ground.

The lock at Gillingham Marina, where tides run hard across the entrance

Sharfleet Creek

There is a sheltered anchorage in relatively deep 'pools' within Sharfleet Creek, where at weekends there is often not very much room. From about 4 hours flood it is possible to wriggle right through the creek and out into Half Acre, passing just south of Beacon No 7 (BW triangle topmark). The whole area is a maze of creeks and saltings and for the first time, passages over drying areas should only be attempted on a flood with frequent soundings.

Middle Reaches

Leaving Stangate for the main river it is desirable to stand well out before turning west in order to pass round the pillar buoy marking the spit at the entrance. Once clear of this all is plain sailing until the river takes its SW'ly turn at Sharp Ness. The passage is well marked with fairway buoys, which are all lit, but a good look-out must be kept, especially at night, for any unlit mooring buoys on the east side of the channel opposite Bee Ness Jetty.

There are two conspicuous jetties in Kethole Reach, Bee Ness and Oakham Ness, both of them used for unloading oil from tankers. Close to the west of the first one - Bee Ness Jetty - is East Hoo Creek which, although uniformly narrow, carries a useful depth of water for about half a mile within its entrance and therefore offers a quiet anchorage except in E'ly or SE'ly winds. No more than two cables north-east of the end of this jetty lies the wreck of Bulwark, marked with one green conical buoy (Fl(3) 15s) and one unlit red can.

Towards the south end of the Kethole Reach opposite Oakham Ness Jetty is the entrance to Half Acre Creek. This broad creek carries 4 to 6 metres at low water for about a mile where it splits into Otterham, Rainham and South Yantlet Creeks, the junction being marked by a red and white Otterham Fairway light buoy flashing the Morse 'A' (−) every 10 seconds. Otterham and Rainham creeks both lead south towards the shore before drying out, but South Yantlet Creek, marked by four unlit spherical buoys (RWVS), joins the main river just south of Darnett Fort, where it dries 0.7m at LWS, although at half tide there will be some 2m over the bar. The best water will be found on a W'ly (mag) course from No 4 buoy (R W V S) with a spherical topmark.

Otterham Creek

The five port and two starboard hand buoys marking the gutway into Otterham Creek are unlit because this narrow channel is little used by commercial traffic nowadays. The quay at the head of the creek was once used by sailing barges to load cement. Now there is a yard and two small shops nearby.

Rainham Creek

Small freighters occasionally use Rainham Creek at HW to reach Bloors Wharf. There is also a little quay near the ruins of Goldsmith's old cement works, the mud for which was dug from the neighbouring marshes and brought to the dock in spritsailed 'muddies'.

The entrance to the creek is marked by a red can light buoy (Fl R (2) 5s), while a couple of unlit red nun buoys mark the gutway farther in.

The main river from the entrance to Half Acre Creek tends westward along Long Reach, where the deep water is hardly more than a quarter of a mile wide. Long Reach is dominated by the buildings and chimneys of Kingsnorth Power Station on the north shore. Three port hand buoys (Nos 18, 20 & 22) mark the south side of the channel along this reach.

Hoo Marsh Passage

Middle Creek which near its entrance provides a useful anchorage, leads through Hoo Flats towards the old wharves near the village of Hoo. The creek is tortuous, but quite well buoyed.

The entrance to the creek is marked with a conical green buoy to be left close to starboard, after which a red can must be left to port and then; turning SW with Gillingham gas holder ahead, another conical green buoy is left to starboard. After turning sharply to the north with Hoo Church ahead, the fourth mark, a yellow and black South Cardinal buoy, is passed on its S side, after which the remaining buoy, a red can, is left to port before reaching either the quays or the marina at Hoo.

This passage should only be attempted on the last hour or so of the flood, until it is known, as the gutways are narrow and very tortuous.

Malcolm Ritman

Port Guide: Gillingham

Gillingham Marina	Tel: 01634 280022 VHF Ch 80
Water	At marina and on pier
Stores	Provisions and off licence at marina; several shops in vicinity. EC Wed
Fuel	Petrol, diesel and gas from marina pontoon; diesel on pier
Repairs Slip	boat hoist and workshop at marina
Transport	Trains to London, Dover, Ramsgate
Telephone	On pier
Club	Medway Cruising Club (Tel: 01634 856489) Can usually supply a mooring for visiting yachtsmen

Middle Creek to Gillingham

At the eastern end of Long Reach, opposite the entrance to Middle Creek, the main river bends to port round Darnett Ness into Pinup Reach. Darnett Ness, on which stands a fort, is marked by a red and white lattice beacon (QR) and is steep on its northern face, but should not be approached too closely on its western side because of a causeway projecting from it. South of this causeway there is anchorage with shelter from easterly winds, near the entrance to South Yantlet Creek.

In Pinup Reach the flood sets sharply towards Folly Point on the starboard hand, on which stands another fort. A rocky spit projecting some 200m from this point is marked by Folly Beacon (B W Con topmark) and no attempt should be made to pass between it and the shore – in fact this corner should be given a wide berth because a spit of mud seems to be extending from it.

Rounding Folly Point into Gillingham Reach, the mud extends some 300 yards from the north shore and the course should be set for the left hand side of the large gas holder at Gillingham until out in mid-stream.

The south side of this reach is lined with the moorings of the Medway Cruising Club, which stands on Gillingham Strand, just east of the gasworks. Landing is possible at the causeway at all states of the tide, or at the pier to the west of the gasworks. At the western end of this reach is the entrance to Chatham Dockyard.

There is a small marina off the end of Gillingham Pier with pontoon berths for some 35 boats with fuel, power and water.

Gillingham Marina

The new, eastern section of Gillingham Marina can accommodate 250 craft and it is accessible through a lock for about four hours each side of HW, but tides run hard across the entrance. The yachts in the older section of the marina can arrive or leave for about two hours before or after each high tide. There are deep water moorings available for arrival or departure at other times. Facilities include repairs, slipway and grid, fuel from pontoon (angled across the run of the tide) outside the lock , chandlery, boat hoist, water and electricity to all pontoons, telephone, showers and 24 hours gate security. (Tel 01634 280022).

The river now turns NW round Hoo Ness into Short Reach, with the high wooded bank of Cockham Reach ahead. Hoo Ness, with a small jetty (two pairs vertical fixed green lights), is steep-to, but to the NW of it a large expanse of mud, covered at half-tide, must be crossed to reach the marina at Hoo.

Hoo

The pontoons and barges of the original floating yacht harbour at Hoo – the first marina to be established on the East Coast – have been rearranged to extend and improve access to the berths, some of which dry out.

Hoo Marina was constructed adjacent to the old harbour, but the new basin is protected by a sill so that there is about 1.5m inside. Usual services are supplied to the finger berths and there are toilets and showers ashore.

The marina can be approached across the mud flats near HW, but can be reached three hours either side of high water (5ft draught) via a creek or gully known locally as the

Port Guide: Hoo

Hoo Marina	Tel: 01634 250311 VHF Ch 80
Water	At marina and Hundred of Hoo SC
Stores	Shops at Hoo village. EC Tues
Fuel	Diesel (own cans) and gas from marina
Repairs	Chandlery and 20 ton crane at marina Slip and crane in W Hoo Creek
Transport	Buses to Rochester
Telephone	Nearby
Clubs	Hoo Ness YC. Hundred of Hoo YC Tel: 01634 250102 (Mooring sometimes available for visitors)

The entrance creek at Hoo Marina is marked by a west cardinal pillar buoy, located just inside a row of mooring buoys north-west of Hoo Ness

The Medway looking to the east above Upnor, with the Medway Yacht Club on the bend of the river below Cockham Woods

Orinoco. Entrance to this gully is almost a mile from the yacht harbours and about half a mile NW of Hoo Ness. The creek mouth is usually marked by a West Cardinal pillar buoy to starboard, to be found just inside a line of large Medway Port Authority mooring buoys and about five orange buoys, connected to assist fore and aft mooring. The latter can be used while waiting for the tide to make.

The Orinoco is marked by posts to be left to port. But the final mark, a small yellow buoy, must be left close to starboard immediately before crossing the sill.

Cockham Reach

The Medway YC at Lower Upnor is situated in Cockham Reach, the prettiest reach on the tidal Medway. The river here is thick with yacht moorings on both sides, three lines on the north shore and a single trot round the bend on the south side. Because it is risky to anchor anywhere near the YC a walk along the foreshore under the woods or a trip in the dinghy will be necessary if a mooring cannot be found. A brief stay (10 min) can be made at the pontoon off the Medway YC. Unfortunately the four-master Arethusa no longer graces the scene. She was sold to the US and can now be seen (as the Peking) at the South Street Seaport Museum, Fulton Street, New York, the Billingsgate of that city.

Above the clubs is Upnor Castle which once guarded the

river against the marauding Dutch fleet. About 2 miles on, round Chatham Ness into Limehouse Reach and Bridge Reach, the river reaches into the busy port of Rochester.

Chatham

The award-winning 80-acre living museum at the Historic Dockyard at Chatham is open during the summer from Wednesday to Sunday, and is well worth a visit. The history of the River Medway can also be recalled by visiting St Mary's Church to see the Medway Heritage Centre.

There is a landing stage at Sun Pier with a telephone and a large chandler nearby. Diesel fuel can be obtained from a barge moored just downstream of the pier.

Many yacht moorings line both sides of the river at Chatham, some belonging to Chatham YC but an increasing number to the Medway Ports Authority. There is a group of clubs based near to Rochester Bridge. The Strood YC can sometimes arrange for a visitor to moor below the bridge, while the Pelican and Rochester Cruising Clubs are on the north and south banks respectively, both above the bridge.

The construction of the Medway River Tunnel, completed in 1995, from near Whitewall Creek to the Dockyard, has resulted in the repositioning of some moorings and the laying of new navigational buoys in the area.

The clearance under Rochester road and rail bridge is approximately 20ft (6m) at HWS. There is not much depth of water at LWS, but the best arch to use is on the starboard side going up river.

Port Guide: Upnor	
Medway YC	Tel: 01634 718399
Water	From clubhouse or Cabin Yacht Stores
Stores	Shop in village nearby (open Sundays)
Fuel	From club
Chandler	Nearby
Transport	Buses to Rochester and Chatham
Clubs	Upnor SC. Medway YC. Wilsonian SC

Port Guide: Rochester	
Water	Shops nearby
Repairs	Boatyard and marine engineer close to pier
Transport	Trains to London, Maidstone, Chatham
Clubs	Rochester Cruising Club. Strood YC

15. The Swale

Tides (Harty Ferry): HW Dover + 1.25 Range: Springs 5.3m Neaps 3.2m
Charts: Admiralty 2571 (East Swale), 2752 (West Swale), Stanford No 5, Imray Y 14
Waypoints: Whitstable Street Buoy 51.23.83N 01.01.70E. Pollard Spit Buoy 51.22.95N 0.58.67E

For ten consecutive editions this section was headed 'The River Swale', but Don Goodsell, who lives at Oare, then pointed out to me that the Swale is not a river and could more correctly be described as a 'ria' – meaning a submerged valley.

Whatever we do call it, it divides the Isle of Sheppey from the mainland of Kent, is seventeen miles in length and follows a tortuous course in a general east-west direction. In ancient days it was the usual route for craft bound for London from the Channel, and it still provides an inside passage between the Medway and the North Kent shore off Whitstable.

The opposing tidal streams meet somewhere near the mouth of Milton Creek. A good time to start through the Swale from W to E, is an hour or so after low water at Sheerness.

The West Swale is entered from the Medway between the drying flats south of Sheerness known as The Lappel, and the extensive Queenborough Spit, the end of which is marked by an E Cardinal Pillar buoy (BYB Q(3) 10s).

The facilities at Queenborough have already been described in Chapter 14 since this anchorage is often thought of as being part of the Medway rather than the Swale.

Loden Hope

Above Queenborough the river turns SW through Loden Hope. Drying mud flats fill the whole of the SE bight from Queenborough hard to the jetty on the NE face of Long Point. A drying horse in mid-stream almost opposite the jetty is marked by a green conical buoy but if the north side is taken, Long Point should be rounded in mid-channel with due regard to mud flats off the north shore.

As the river turns south along Long Reach the best water is towards the west side of mid-channel.

About a mile after Long Point (in Horse Reach) two prominent cable notice boards will be seen on NE bank. Abreast of these, there is a small horse practically in mid-channel. This is marked by two red can buoys and should be passed on its SW side about one-third of river width off the Kent shore.

There are two sets of leading marks, with lights to assist boats through Horse Reach. The first pair of marks and lights (flashing green) are on the south bank and provide a leading line of 120°M while the second pair, bearing 105°M are located on the west bank and flash red.

From Horse Reach, Kingsferry Bridge spanning the river is seen ahead. Although here the river is narrow, and carries quite large ships, small craft can usually find temporary anchorage on the SW shore just by the bridge. This is also the best spot for landing from a dinghy as the surface is hard.

Kingsferry Bridge will open to permit vessels with fixed masts to pass on request, provided always that railway traffic permits. If a train is on the line between Sittingbourne and

Kingsferry Bridge, with Ridham Dock in the foreground and the western entrance to the Swale in the distance

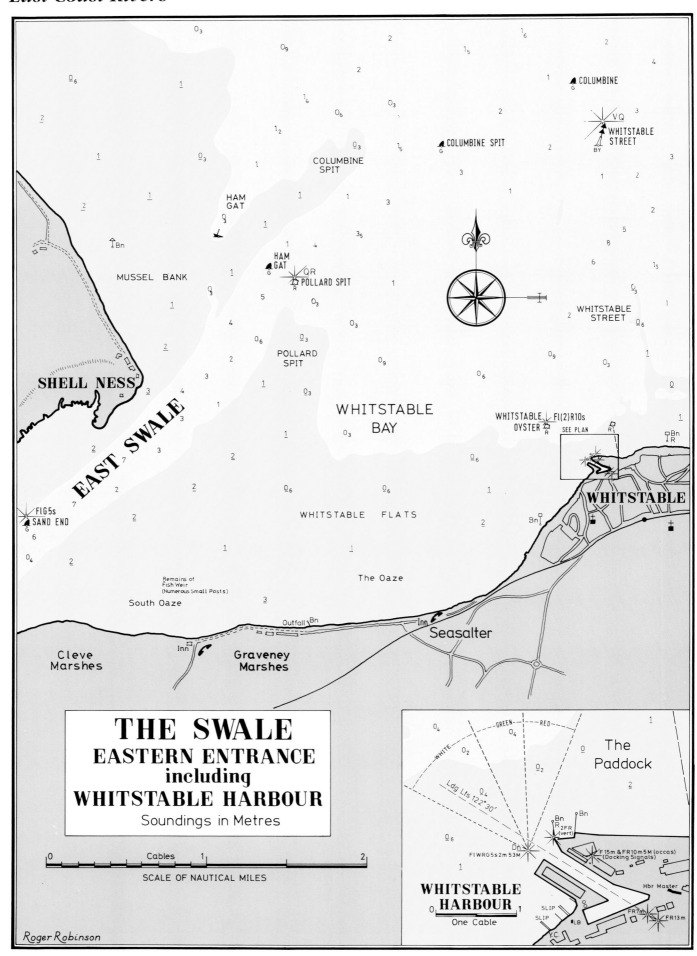

THE SWALE
EASTERN ENTRANCE
including
WHITSTABLE HARBOUR
Soundings in Metres

Cables

SCALE OF NAUTICAL MILES

WHITSTABLE
HARBOUR
One Cable

Roger Robinson

Malcolm Ritman

The Kingsferry railway bridge over the River Swale will be opened on request, train timetables permitting

Sheerness, the bridge may not be opened and do not be surprised if this sometimes results in a wait of half an hour or so.

Two more lights, on the W bank near Ridham Dock serve to lead ships through the bridge, the front is 2 F G and the rear 2 F W on a line of 155°M. Sets of six 'traffic lights' are displayed on the south buttress of the bridge, near the bridge-keeper's cabin. The lights are grouped in two vertical lines of three, the top pair white, middle pair orange, and lowest pair green.

The accepted signals for a yacht to give when wishing to pass through the bridge is to hoist a bucket in the rigging, or one long and four short 'toots'.

When both green and red lights are flashing, the bridge is about to be lifted. When fixed green lights are shown it has been fully raised. Flashing red lights indicate that the span is being lowered. A flashing orange light indicates that the bridge is not working and craft should keep clear. If no lights at all are shown, then nothing will happen because the bridge is shut down.

The height clearance with the span raised is 27m at LWOS. The width between the bascules is also 27m. Tidal streams run strongly; from 3 to 4kn on the first flood and first of ebb.

Just beyond the bridge on the SW shore is Ridham Dock, used by large coasting vessels for which look-out should be kept around high water when they may leave via the bridge.

Two port- and two starboard-hand light buoys have been established in Ferry and Clay Reaches between Ridham Dock and Grovehurst Jetty, where the channel is no more than half a cable wide at LW.

A little over half a mile farther east is the nominal point at which the two tidal streams meet (see later). The river then turns to the east past a modern jetty on the west shore, the entrance to Milton Creek, which may be considered the end of the western half of the Swale.

Ridham dock is purely commercial serving the large paper mills nearby and usually occupied by sizeable freighters.

Milton Creek

This area is likely to be of greatest interest to industrial archaeologists who may wish to visit the Dolphin Yard barge museum at Sittingbourne; but even they may be well advised to get there by road rather than via the creek. (The museum is usually open on Sundays and Bank Holidays from Easter to mid October.

East Swale

The approach from seaward commences at the Columbine buoy (Con G) about 2½ miles north of Whitstable Town, but from this distance the precise entrance to the Swale is not easily recognised. A course of 235°M passing along the SE edge of the Columbine Shoal, leaving the Columbine Spit buoy (Con G) to starboard will lead to the next visible marks in about a mile. The Pollard Spit light buoy (Can R QR should be left to port and the Ham Gat buoy (Con G) to starboard. The Pollard Spit extends north from Whitstable Flats, an area of sand and mud to the east of Whitstable.

From a point midway between Ham Gat and Pollard Spit buoys a course 220°M leads into the river, passing Shell Ness to starboard about a quarter of a mile off. Cottages and coastguard buildings are conspicuous above its light-coloured shell shingle beach, and in conditions of poor visibility Shell Ness is a useful check on distance from the next mark – the Sand End buoy (Con G FlG 5s) about a mile away on the same course.

Whitstable Flats and the Swale entrance are an oyster fishery area, and care should be taken not to anchor or ground on the oyster beds.

Once inside the river entrance the tides set fairly but at the

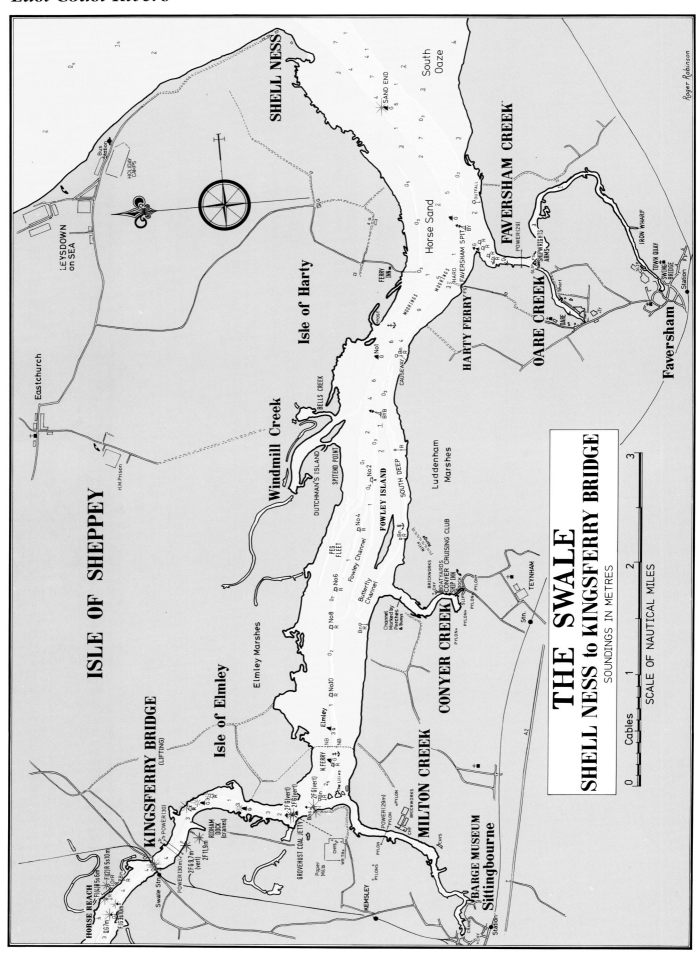

THE SWALE
SHELL NESS to KINGSFERRY BRIDGE
SOUNDINGS IN METRES

Although the causeway is known as Harty Ferry, no ferry now operates between the mainland and the Isle of Sheppey

entrance they are affected to some extent by the main Thames Estuary streams, and there is a tendency for vessels entering on the flood to be set over towards the Columbine; while leaving on the ebb, the set is towards Pollard Spit.

Throughout this long entrance the width of the channel is between two and three cables up to the Sand End buoy, after which the channel narrows.

Next there is a pair of unlit buoys off the entrance to Faversham Creek. The one to the starboard marks the south side of the Horse Shoal while the other (N Card BY) is on the end of the spit extending from the north bank of the creek.

Immediately to the west is Harty Ferry, the most popular anchorage in the Swale. The ferry no longer operates but the hard on the north shore provides access to the Ferry House Inn. A favourite berth (except during strong easterlies) is under the north shore near the hard, but beware the fierce current on the early ebb, particularly at night. This can be a dangerous anchorage with strong winds from the east.

Harty Ferry

There are few facilities available to the boats moored at Harty Ferry, although water can be obtained from a spring on the south shore near the hard, or from the Inn on the north shore, where yachtsmen are welcomed. There is an emergency telephone near the top of the ferry hard on the south bank. For other services and stores the nearest places are Oare (1 mile) or Faversham (2 miles).

West from Harty a green conical buoy half a mile ahead should not be approached too closely, as in SW winds it wanders well up over the mud.

From here on the channel shoals and becomes narrower. Ahead to port will be seen the higher parts of Fowley Island, a long shoal parallel to the Kent shore, marked by an E Cardinal buoy, behind which lies South Deep.

The E Cardinal Fowley Spit buoy is not too easy to pick out, but the spit is long and shoals steeply to the south, so a careful watch must be kept on the depth.

The main channel, which soon narrows to little more than half a cable, leaves Fowley to port, and lies approximately midway between the north edge of Fowley and the Sheppey shore. Passing Fowley Island the only guides are four port-hand buoys, and then, further west, two green conicals, Swale no.10 and Elmley, which indicate the best water. The channel

is, however, so narrow that a fair wind is essential anywhere near low water.

Farther west, two posts mark the hards of Elmley Ferry, where James II boarded a boat in 1688, and fled the country. The hards extend well off-shore beyond the posts and that off the south shore has some stakes embedded in it. The best water lies a trifle to north of a line midway between the posts. The ferry no longer functions but the remains of the Ferry House can be seen on the south bank.

Anchorage

Just west of Elmley Ferry, on the mainland side, there is space to anchor, out of the fairway, in about 1½ fathoms.

From here, the river swings round towards the north between the green conical N Ferry and the red can S Ferry buoys, passing a patch of saltings that largely masks the entrance to Milton Creek. The best water will be found more or less in a direct line towards Grovehurst jetty, which shows 2 FG lights at night. The old Lilies beacon at the entrance to Milton Creek has been replaced by The Lilies buoy (black and yellow S. Cardinal with black topmark) on the north side of the river.

Past Milton Creek, the banks of the river are closer together, and the good water now occupies about a third of the available river width. Although there are few marks to assist, it is fairly easy to negotiate this part of the river as there is appreciably more water than in the eastern end.

Remember that the direction of buoyage and marking changes here, off Milton Creek.

The East Swale Creeks

Faversham

Faversham Creek branches off to the south of the Swale just east of Harty Ferry and is marked at its entrance with a N Cardinal (BY) buoy, to be left to starboard when entering. Sometimes there is also a port hand buoy or beacon at the entrance to keep boats off the mud on the east side of the channel.

The creek itself pursues a winding course for about 3½ miles up to the town of Faversham. For the first half mile up to the junction with Oare Creek (to starboard) the channel is fairly wide and well marked with port and starboard buoys.

In behind the seawall at Hollow Shore is the Shipwright's

Conyer Creek looking towards the yard and the quayside

Arms, a pub with character but without mains electricity, gas or water. The yard nearby is always interesting because of the traditional craft that congregate there. The services at the yard are those that relate to repairs and maintenance: a slip, a crane and a dock.

Landing is possible near the inn from about four hours before to four hours after HW. Shallow draught boats can lie afloat throughout a neap tide off the inn, but remember that Faversham Creek is often used by commercial craft and a few sailing barges.

Above the junction, Faversham Creek narrows and dries right out. In the absence of buoys, the deepest water is to be found in the centre of the creek. Barges and oil tankers work up to Faversham on the tide; so shoal-draught craft with power can make the trip, starting about four hours flood.

The first yard to be reached will be at Standard Quay, on the south shore. There are extensive alongside moorings here and, just as at Hollow Shore, there are always interesting craft to be seen. The services are largely aimed at DIY enthusiasts but include water, power and diesel fuel as well as a dry dock large enough to take a Thames barge. Further up the creek and on the opposite bank there is a yard re-occupying the site of the original Faversham shipyard. Finally, there is a third yard with pontoon moorings just below the bridge and almost in the town itself.

Oare Creek

It is about a mile to the village of Oare which can be reached around HW by boats requiring up to 2m of water by way of a creek marked by withies. There are stages with boats moored to them practically all the way along the SE bank of Oare Creek, while at the head of the creek drying pontoons have been constructed to form a small marina within a few yards of the road to Faversham.

Conyer Creek

There are two ways into Conyer Creek from the South Deep inside Fowley Island. Coming from the east (Harty Ferry), the East Cardinal buoy at the end of Fowley Spit is left to starboard, before following a line of moorings, past a green 'nun' buoy with topmark and then a red 'nun' buoy, up to a pair of withies marking the entrance to Conyer Creek. Leave the one with a triangle topmark close to starboard and then follow the sequence of starboard-hand withies that lead close to the sea wall near the old Butterfly Wharf. Thereafter, pairs of withies with triangular or disc topmarks will lead you, if there is enough water, round the outside of the bends and up to Conyer village.

The second way into Conyer Creek is via a gulley known as the Butterfly channel. Shoal draught craft approaching from the west (Queenborough) can, starting from No 8 buoy in the main channel, turn SE and sound across the spit off the western end of Fowley Island into the deeper water of South Deep. A pair of perches indicate the entrance to the Butterfly channel which at first leads close under the sea wall on the

Port Guide: Oare and Hollow Shore	
Water	From yards at Oare and Hollow Shore
Stores	From shop at Oare
Chandler	At Oare
Fuel	Diesel from yards
Repairs	Yards at Oare and Hollow Shore. Slipways. Crane up to 5 tons at Hollow Shore and 15 tons at Oare
Transport	Bus from Oare to Faversham
Club	Hollow Shore Cruising Club Tel: 01795 533254

Port Guide: Conyer	
Conyer Marine	Tel: 01795 521711
Swale Marine	Tel 01795 521562
Water	Laid on at boatyards
Stores	From chandler
Repairs	Two yards, with slipways, boat lift and cranes.
Sailmaker	At quayside
Fuel	Diesel at yards
Transport	Bus service to Teynham and Sittingbourne. Trains to London, Dover and Ramsgate from Teynham or Sittingbourne
Club	Conyer CC

Malcolm Ritman

The winding channel leading up to the yards at Conyer is marked partly by withies and partly by buoys

western side of the entrance, but then turns abruptly to the east before reaching Conyer Creek itself at a junction marked with a perch bearing a double triangle topmark.

There are two yards at Conyer, both offering complete services to yachtsmen, most of the berths are alongside drying pontoons.

Conyer Marine will keep a VHF watch if requested and will guide boats into the creek from South Deep.

Windmill Creek

Runs off to the north about one mile west of Harty Ferry. The spit off its western side is marked with a post. It formerly ran some miles inland, but it has now been blocked and is of little interest except to wildfowlers.

Whitstable Harbour

This small harbour lies two or three miles east of the entrance to the East Swale. It is controlled by Canterbury Council and is used regularly by small freighters and by local fishing boats and barges, but it offers shelter to yachtsmen who are prevented from making the Thames or Medway during a westerly or south-westerly blow. Berthing for yachts is, however,

temporary and at the discretion of the harbourmaster. The narrow entrance to the harbour can be reached only over the shoal water that extends for more than a mile off-shore. Best approach is from a position about a mile W of the Whitstable Street buoy (N Card VQ) on a course of 170° M held until within half a mile of the harbour entrance by which time, if it is dark, the Whitstable 'Oyster' buoy (Can R Fl(2)R 10s) will be seen on the starboard bow while continuing on the same course within the green sector of a flashing light on the W Quay dolphin just off the harbour entrance. This dolphin and a conspicuous tall granary building provide useful daylight marks. The light on the dolphin has WR and G sectors and flashes every 5 seconds. The white sector serves shoal draught boats approaching from the west, while the red sector is to keep craft off a shoal called Whitstable Street. There are leading lights (FR) into the harbour on a bearing of 130° M.

Swale Tides

Tidal streams are peculiar because of the two outlets to the sea. At LW Sheerness it is slack water almost throughout the Swale. As the flood commences, it naturally enters from both ends, the streams meeting at about Fowley, or even as far west as Elmley on very high tides. At HW Sheerness it is slack throughout the Swale, and for the first hour after HW the whole body of water moves eastward, when at about Long Point the westerly stream turns right round and ebbs back into the Medway; while the remainder of the water continues to move to the east. As the ebb continues, the point of separation of the stream also moves eastwards, until ultimately the separation occurs near Fowley.

As the result of this there is an east-going stream for about nine hours every tide at Elmley; while at Kingsferry Bridge the tide sets to the east for eight hours. By the time Harty is reached the duration of east and west-going streams is about six hours each, but it is sometimes useful to know that on the north side of the West Swale there is a west-going eddy for as much as an hour before the ebb stops flowing eastward on the south side of the river.

The early ebb is strong, until the banks are uncovered, approaching 3 or 4 knots at Kingsferry.

In the East Swale, tides are considerably affected by prevailing winds, easterlies causing the higher levels.

Port Guide: Whitstable	
Harbourmaster	01227 274086
VHF	Channels 16,12 or 9 from 0800 to 1700 (Mon-Fri) or any day from 3 hrs before and 2 hrs after HW
Water	Alongside at Harbour
Stores	Shops in town. EC Wed
Chandler	Nearby
Petrol and oil	Garages nearby
Repairs	Several yards with slipways, and sailmaker
Transport	Train service to London (Victoria)
Harbour dues	Check with HM (Tel: Whitstable 0227 274086)
Customs Office	At Harbour
Club	At Whitstable Yacht Club. (Tel 272343 or 272942). (Can sometimes offer a mooring)

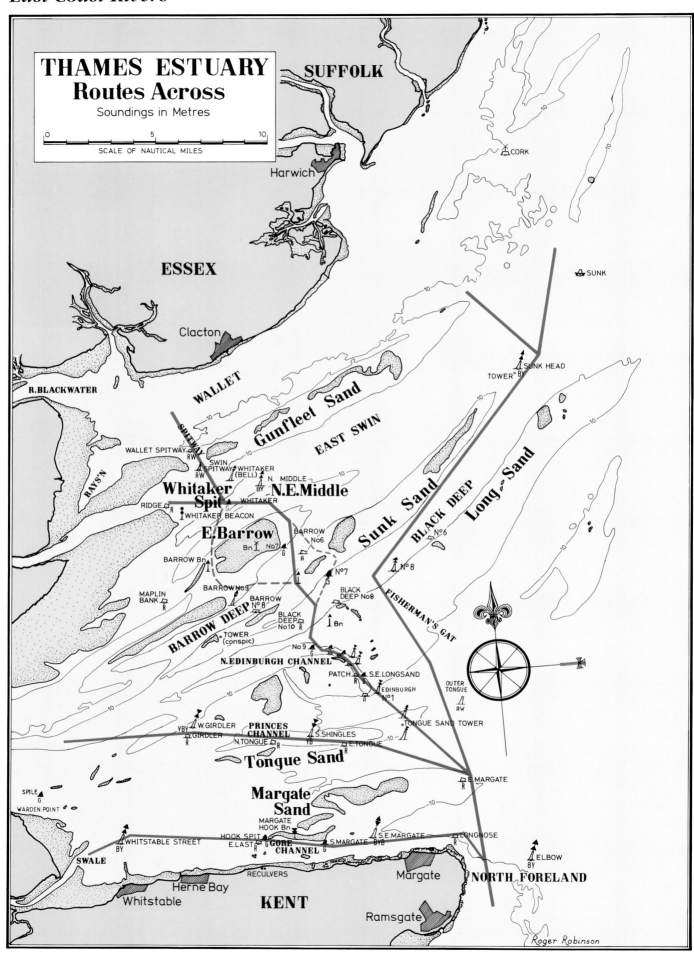

THAMES ESTUARY
Routes Across
Soundings in Metres

SCALE OF NAUTICAL MILES

SUFFOLK

Harwich

ESSEX

Clacton

R.BLACKWATER

CORK

SUNK

WALLET

Gunfleet Sand

EAST SWIN

SUNK HEAD
TOWER° BY

RAYS'N

SPITWAY

WALLET SPITWAY
RW

SWIN
SPITWAY WHITAKER
RW (BELL)

N. MIDDLE

Whitaker
Spit

N.E.Middle

RIDGE
R

WHITAKER

WHITAKER BEACON

E.Barrow

BARROW
No6

Sunk Sand

BLACK DEEP

Long Sand

No6

Bn
No7
G

R

Nº8

BARROW Bn

No7
G

MAPLIN
BANK
R

BARROW No9
R

BARROW
Nº8
R

Nº Bn

BLACK
DEEP No8

FISHERMAN'S GAT

BLACK
DEEP
No10 R

Bn

BARROW DEEP

TOWER
(conspic)

No 9
G

N.EDINBURGH CHANNEL

PATCH
R

S.E.LONGSAND
G

EDINBURGH
Nº1
R

OUTER
TONGUE
RW

W.GIRDLER
YBY
GIRDLER
R

PRINCES
CHANNEL

N.TONGUE
R

S.SHINGLES
YB

E.TONGUE
R

Tongue Sand

Tongue Sand Tower

E.MARGATE
R

SPILE
G
WARDEN POINT

Margate
Sand

MARGATE
HOOK Bn

LONGNOSE
R

WHITSTABLE STREET
BY

HOOK SPIT

E.LAST
BY

GORE
CHANNEL

S.MARGATE
BYB

S.E.MARGATE

ELBOW
BY

SWALE

RECULVERS

Margate

NORTH FORELAND

Herne Bay

Whitstable

KENT

Ramsgate

Roger Robinson

16. Cross-Estuary Routes

There is a story by Archie White in which an old West Mersea barge skipper tells a young fellow with his first command how he can sneak through the Rays'n, past the Ridge Buoy (where it used to be) over the top of the Whitaker Spit and out into the Swin off Shoebury; thereby reaching the London River well ahead of all the other barges that had been storm-bound with him in the Blackwater.

It is a good story and probably true, because it certainly is possible to cut many corners by using the swatchways in the Thames Estuary.

Precautions

Before any yachtsman sets out to cross the shoal infested mouth of the Thames, he must give careful consideration to a number of things that may not have seemed important to him during short distance cruising between adjacent rivers within sight of land. They are:

1. Corrected Compass If visibility should close in when half way across, a reliable compass will be essential.

2. Corrected Charts A copy of *East Coast Rivers*, even if it is the latest edition, is not adequate for crossing the Thames Estuary. Admiralty chart No 1183 will be necessary and must be corrected up to date. Even then it must always be remembered that during the several years that often elapse between surveys carried out by the PLA Hydrographic Department of a particular area, significant changes often take place, particularly in the very swatchways that are of special interest to yachtsmen. For this reason a reliable echo-sounder will be indispensable.

3. Tidal information Work out and understand what the tide will be doing at all important points along the route – not only at the time you hope to be there, but also for later times in case you are delayed. For this purpose the tidal diagrams included will be useful, although the larger scale Tidal Stream Atlas (No 249) published by the Admiralty will be even better. Remember that depths will vary according to direction and strength of wind and barometric pressure – tidal predictions are just that.

4. Waypoints Prepare a list of all waypoints that might prove useful.

Weather Forecast

The latest possible weather forecast for the area must be obtained for a period at least twice as long as the time the passage is expected to take.

Some useful numbers are:

London Weather Centre 0171 242 3663
Telecom Marinecall 0891 500 455 or VHF Ch 02

Emergency Equipment

Ensure the adequacy of emergency equipment, including: VHF, flares/smoke signals, life-jackets, liferaft/dinghy.

Conditions in the Estuary

Since the passage across the Estuary will generally be made during the SW-going flood tide, it must be realised that when the wind is from the SW, as it so often is, then a short

and very steep sea gets up in anything more than a moderate breeze.

For many of us, the first time we find ourselves in command of a yacht out of sight of land is when we set out from one or other of the Essex or Suffolk rivers and proceed seaward beyond the Spitway and the Whitaker Bell buoy or round the NE Gunfleet. The distance across the Thames Estuary between, say, Clacton and the North Foreland is about 25 miles, so we should not be surprised that it feels different out there amidst the shoals when the buoys don't come up as soon as we would like.

Swin Spitway or Whitaker Buoy to North Foreland

Waypoints: Whitaker buoy to North Foreland

BARROW No 7 buoy 51.38.19N 01.14.20E
SW Sunk Beacon 51.36.32N 01.14.90E
N EDINBURGH No 9 buoy 51.33.46N 01.16.70E
N EDINBURGH No 1 buoy 51.31.44N 01.21.67E
TONGUE SAND TOWER (N) buoy 51.29.60N 01.22.12E
E MARGATE buoy 51.27.00N 01.26.50E

There was a time when almost anyone crossing the Estuary passed from the East Swin into the Barrow Deep through a swatchway opposite Barrow No 9 buoy; but No 9 buoy has been moved a mile or so SW and no longer marks the entrance to the swatch. This route can still be taken provided it is realised that there is very little water just north of the Barrow Beacon. A narrow shoal extends for about two miles in a SW'ly direction from the NW side of the East Barrow Sand and the way through into the Middle Deep passes close north of the beacon and over a ridge with less than 1m at LWS.

Alternative routes

Another possible route passes north of the E Barrow Sand and into the Barrow Deep that way. From close north of the Ridge (CanR) or the S Whitaker (ConG) buoy, shape an E'ly (°M) course to pass about a mile south of the N Middle (N Cardinal) buoy until Barrow No 7 buoy (Con G FlG 2.5s) bears S (°M). Then, with the sounder going, skirt round the NE edge of the East Barrow Sand to leave Barrow No 7 close to starboard. Another mile on a S'ly course will bring the SW Sunk Beacon in view, and this should be passed close to, on a course of 135°M (with the NW Longsand Bn ahead about three miles away), until deep water is found in the Black Deep. When safely through the swatch, change course to leave Black Deep No 10 buoy (Can R Fl(2)R 5s) a quarter of a mile to starboard.

In recent years there has been a swatchway with 4 metres least water about 2 cables NE of the SW Sunk beacon, but Admiralty charts Nos 1975 or 1183 will show current configurations of these shoals. It is not safe to pass on a direct line between No 6 buoy in the Barrow Deep and No 7 buoy in the Black Deep.

From abreast Black Deep No 10 it should be possible to see No 9 and then No 7 green conical buoys in the western entrance to the North Edinburgh Channel.

The North Edinburgh Channel is marked on both sides with buoys at intervals of a mile or less and, apart from keeping out of the way of any big ships which sometimes come up astern surprisingly quickly, it should present no problem. However, because the buoyage in the North Edinburgh Channel is changed quite frequently, it is essential to have Chart No 1183 fully corrected and up to date and to keep to the north of No 4 red can buoy, because the shoal it guards is extremely steep-to.

After emerging from the North Edinburgh Channel, the Tongue Sand Tower buoys will provide useful marks from which to shape a course (about 140°M) to the East Margate buoy (Can R FlR 2.5s) and then on to the North Foreland.

The Tide

In order to make most of the passage on a rising tide it will be necessary to be near the Whitaker Bell buoy just before low water – which is rather convenient for those leaving the Crouch but does mean that those coming through the Spitway will have to be careful. The aim is to get into the Barrow Deep just as the flood starts running SW'ly and then, by making an average of 4 or 5 knots over the ground, reach the North Edinburgh Channel while there is some E going tide to help and a chance to reach the Foreland before the N going stream starts, about an hour before HW Dover.

When crossing the Estuary for the first time from Dover or Ramsgate, it will be best to stem the last of the south going tide up the North Foreland so as to get the benefit of the flood through the North Edinburgh Channel and across the Estuary. Unfortunately, this usually means arriving at the entrance to the Crouch or the Spitway at about HW, with the prospect of the whole of the ebb to run out of the Essex rivers. The only way this can be avoided is to take the risks involved in crossing the Estuary on a falling tide – *which certainly cannot be recommended for the inexperienced.*

Harwich to North Foreland

Waypoints
Harwich to North Foreland
SUNK HEAD TOWER buoy 51.46.60N 01.30.60E
BLACK DEEP No 8 buoy 51.36.20N 01.20.00E
OUTER TONGUE buoy 51.30.70N 01.26.50E

Those wishing to cross the Estuary from the Suffolk rivers need not use the Wallet and the Spitway, but can enter the Black Deep past the ruined Sunk Head Tower, marked by its N Cardinal buoy (N Card Q), and then after proceeding about 10 miles to the SW, leave the Black Deep via the Fisherman's Gat and then proceed to the Outer Tongue buoy (RW Fl 10s Whis). There is 5 or 6 metres of water in the Fisherman's Gat at LWS and the swatch is entered about a mile and a half E of the Black Deep No 7 buoy (Con G QG) and an equal distance SW of Black Deep No 6 buoy (West Cardinal Q (a) 15s). Unfortunately, since the Navaid Review, there is no nearer buoy from which to locate the swatchway.

Thames, Medway or Swale to North Foreland
Waypoints
W GIRDLER buoy 51.29.58N 01.06.82E
S SHINGLES buoy 51.29.20N 01.16.12E
TONGUE SAND TOWER (N) buoy 51.29.60N 01.22.12E
SPILE buoy 51.26.40N 00.55.80E

There are various routes that can be taken in a W-E direction along the north coast of Kent, but in general craft from the Thames or the Medway will tend to use the Princes Channel, about five miles offshore, while those coming from the Swale or Whitstable are more likely to go through the Gore Channel, much closer inshore. The historic 'Overland' route from Thames to North Foreland departs from the Medway Channel, near Nos 4 or 6 buoys, on a course to the Spile buoy (G Con Fl G 2.5s). Whence via the Horse Channel to the East Last and Hook Spit buoys at the entrance to the Gore Channel off Reculver.

Prince's Channel
Waypoints
GIRDLER buoy 51.29.16N 01.06.50E
SE GIRDLER buoy 51.29.47N 01.10.00E
S SHINGLES Bell buoy 51.29.20N 01.16.12E

The Prince's Channel can be said to commence between the Girdler (Can R Fl(4)R 15s) and the W Girdler (W Card Q(9) 15s Bell) buoys and to continue in an easterly direction past the SE Girdler (Con G Fl(3) G 10s) for about five miles between the South Shingles shoal to the north and the Ridge and the Tongue Sands to the south. At its narrowest point, abreast the North Tongue buoy (Can R Fl(3) R 10s), the deep water is almost a mile wide. From this position, an E'ly (mag) course will lead past the South Shingles (S Card Q(6) & LFl 15s) and the East Tongue (Can R Fl(2) R 5s) buoys, by which time the N and S Cardinal Tongue Sand Tower buoys should be in sight pretty well straight ahead. When these buoys are close abeam, a course can be laid, (about 150°M), to clear the Foreland after leaving the East Margate (Can R Fl(2) R 2.5s) about half a mile to starboard.

Gore Channel
Waypoints
WHITSTABLE STREET buoy 51.23.83N 01.01.70E
HOOK SPIT buoy 51.24.05N 01.12.65E
S MARGATE buoy 51.23.88N 01.16.75E
SE MARGATE buoy 51.24.10N 01.20.50E
LONGNOSE SPIT buoy 51.23.90N 01.25.85E

This route is closer inshore and rather more difficult because of the many drying shoals off the Kent coast between Herne Bay and Margate.

Starting from the Whitstable Street buoy (N Card VQ) a course of 95°M will lead (after about 6 miles) to the East Last (Can R QR) and Hook Spit (Can G) buoys marking the narrow swatch over the western end of the Margate Hook Sand. Because of rocky patches off the Reculvers, do not approach the shore closer than two miles or proceed eastwards until these two marks have been found. The twin rectangular towers of the Reculvers will help in locating the buoys.

Once through the swatch, shape a course of 110°M to leave the Margate Hook Beacon (S Card Topmark) and the South Margate buoy (Can G FlG 2.5s) at least a quarter of a mile to the North. From the South Margate buoy an E'ly (mag) course will lead to the SE Margate buoy (E Card Q(3) 10s) a little more than two miles away. The passage can then be continued to round the Longnose buoy (N Card VQ) about a mile offshore.

Tidal Constants

Place		Add (+) to or Subtract (-) from times of HW at:		Height relative to Chart Datum (metres)			
				SPRINGS		NEAPS	
		Dover	Harwich	MHW	MLW	MHW	MLW
1 Southwold		-1.05	-1.45	2.4	0.5	2.1	1.0
2 Orford River	Orford Haven (Entrance)	+0.15	-0.25	3.2	0.3	2.6	0.9
	Orford Quay	+1.00	+0.35	2.4	0.4	2.1	1.3
3 River Alde	Slaughden Quay (Aldeburgh)	+1.55	+1.00	2.9	0.4	2.4	1.3
	Snape Bridge	+2.55	+2.00	2.9	0.8	2.4	0.8
4 River Deben	Woodbridge Haven (Entrance)	+0.25	-0.10	3.7	0.5	2.9	1.0
	Waldringfield	+1.00	+0.20	3.6	0.4	3.0	0.9
	Woodbridge	+1.05	+0.30	3.8	0.4	3.1	0.9
5 Harwich Harbour	Harwich	+0.50	–	4.0	0.4	3.4	1.1
6 River Orwell	Pin Mill	+1.00	+0.10	4.1	0.4	3.4	1.1
	Ipswich	+1.15	+0.20	4.2	0.3	3.4	1.0
7 River Stour	Wrabness	+1.05	+0.15	4.1	0.4	3.4	1.1
	Mistley	+1.15	+0.25	4.2	0.3	3.4	1.0
8 Walton Backwaters	Walton-on-Naze (Pier)	+0.30	-0.05	4.2	0.4	3.4	1.1
	Stone Point	+0.40	+0.05	4.1	0.5	3.3	1.2
9 River Colne	Colne Point	+0.40	+0.10	5.1	0.4	3.8	1.2
	Brightlingsea	+0.50	+0.15	5.0	0.4	3.8	1.2
	Wivenhoe	+1.05	+0.25	4.9	0.3	3.6	–
	Colchester (The Hythe)	+1.15	+0.35	4.2	–	3.1	–
10 River Blackwater	Bench Head Buoy	+1.20	+0.40	5.1	0.5	3.8	1.2
	West Mersea (Nass Beacon)	+1.10	+0.30	5.1	0.5	3.8	1.2
	Tollesbury Mill Creek	+1.00	+0.20	4.9	–	3.6	–
	Bradwell Quay	+1.10	+0.30	5.3	0.5	4.2	1.3
	Osea Island	+1.25	+0.45	5.3	0.4	4.3	1.2
	Heybridge Basin	+1.30	+0.50	5.0	–	4.1	–
	Maldon	+1.35	+0.55	2.9	–	2.3	–
11 River Crouch	Whitaker Beacon	+0.50	+0.15	4.8	0.5	3.9	1.3
	Burnham-on-Crouch	+1.15	+0.40	5.2	0.2	4.2	1.0
	Fambridge	+1.20	+0.40	5.3	0.3	4.2	1.1
	Hullbridge	+1.25	+0.45	5.3	0.3	4.2	1.1
12 River Roach	Paglesham	+1.10	+0.30	5.2	0.2	4.2	1.0
	Havengore Creek	+1.10	+0.25	4.2	0.4	3.4	1.1
13 River Thames	Southend Pier	+1.20	+0.40	5.8	0.5	4.7	1.4
	Holehaven	+1.30	+0.50	5.9	0.4	4.7	1.4
	Gravesend	+1.45	+1.05	6.3	0.3	4.7	1.4
	Erith	+2.00	+1.20	6.6	0.1	4.9	1.2
	Tower Bridge	+2.40	+2.55	6.8	0.5	5.9	1.3
14 The Medway	Queenborough	+1.35	+0.55	5.7	0.6	4.8	1.5
	Rochester	+1.50	+1.10	5.9	0.3	5.0	1.3
15 The Swale	Whitstable	+1.20	+0.40	5.5	0.5	4.4	1.5
	Harty Ferry	+1.25	+0.45	5.7	0.6	5.1	1.2
	Milton Creek	+1.35	+0.55	5.7	0.6	4.8	0.5

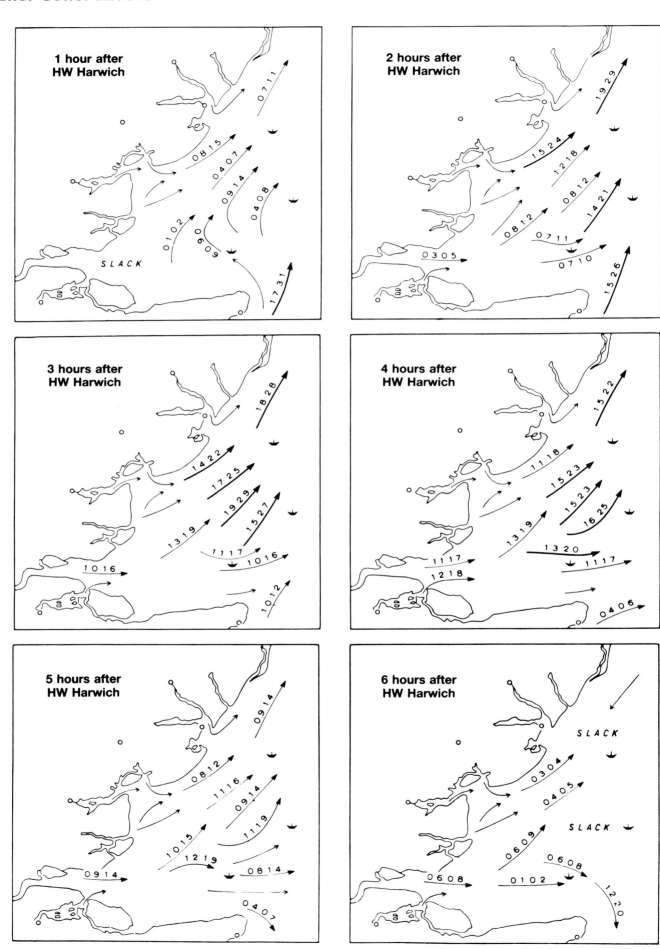

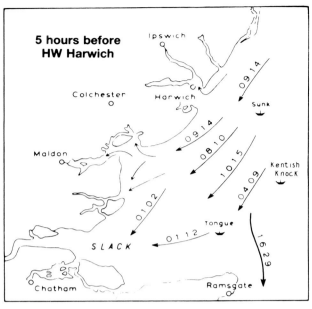

5 hours before HW Harwich

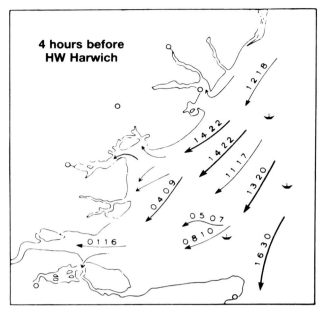

4 hours before HW Harwich

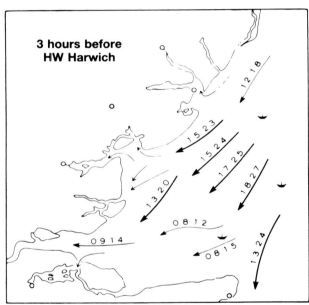

3 hours before HW Harwich

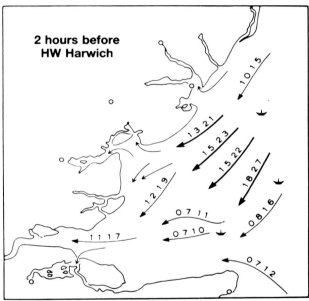

2 hours before HW Harwich

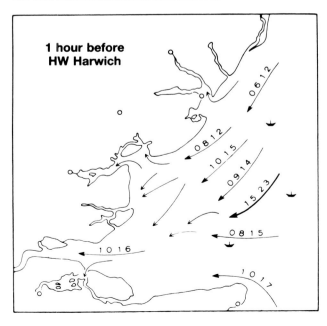

1 hour before HW Harwich

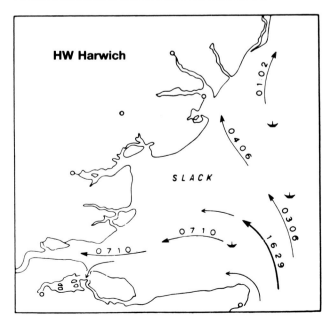

HW Harwich

Navigable Distances (Approximate)

River Thames		Sea Miles
Sea Reach No 1 Buoy to	Southend Pier	6
	Sheerness	5
	Holehaven	11
	Gravesend	19
	Erith	25
	Greenwich	35
	London Bridge	41
Southend Pier to	Sheerness	6
	Havengore entrance	9½
	Leigh (Bell Wharf)	3
	Benfleet	6½

River Medway		
Sheerness (Garrison Pt) to	Queenborough	1½
	Gillingham	8
	Upnor	10½
	Rochester Bridge	12½

River Swale		
Queenborough to	Kingsferry Bridge	2
	Harty Ferry	9
	Columbine Buoy	15

River Crouch		
Whitaker Beacon to	Foulness	7
	Roach Entrance	9½
	Burnham	12
Burnham to	Fambridge	5
	Hullbridge	7
	Battlesbridge	9
Foulness to	Bench Head Buoy (via Ray Sand)	8
	Bench Head Buoy (via Spitway)	18

River Roach		
Entrance to	Paglesham	4
	Havengore Bridge	5

River Blackwater		
Bench Head Buoy to	Sales Point	4
	Nass Beacon (West Mersea)	5
	Bradwell Quay	6
	Osea Island	10
	Heybridge Basin	13
	Maldon (Hythe)	14½

River Colne		Sea Miles
Colne Bar Buoy to	Brightlingsea	4½
	Wivenhoe	8
	Colchester (Hythe)	11

The Wallet		
Knoll Lightbuoy to	Clacton Pier	4
	Walton-on-the-Naze (Pier)	9
	Stone Banks Buoy	12½
	Harwich Entrance	15

Harwich		
Harbour Entrance to	Burnham (via Wallet and Spitway)	30
	West Mersea (via Wallet)	23
	Brightlingsea (via Wallet)	22
	Woodbridge Haven (Deben Entrance)	6
	Orford Haven (Ore Entrance)	10

River Stour		
Harwich Harbour to (Entrance)	Wrabness	6½
	Mistley	9½
	Manningtree	11

River Orwell		
Harwich Harbour to (Entrance)	Pin Mill	6½
	Ipswich	11

River Deben		
Entrance to (Felixstowe Ferry)	Ramsholt	3
	Waldringfield	5½
	Woodbridge	9

River Ore		
Entrance to (Shingle Street)	Havergate I	3
	Orford Quay	5

River Alde		
Orford Quay to	Slaughden Quay (Aldeburgh)	
	Iken Cliff	8½
	Snape Bridge	11
Southwold to	Orford Haven	20
	Harwich Harbour	30

Glossary

ENGLISH	DUTCH	FRENCH	GERMAN
Abeam	Dwars	Par le travers	Querab
Ahead	Vooruit	En avant	Voraus
Anchorage	Ankerplaats	Mouillage	Ankerplatz
Astern	Achteruit	En arrière	Ruckwarts, achtern
Athwart	Dwars over	Par le travers	Aufwaschen
Bank	Bank	Banc	Bank
Bar	Drempel	Barre	Drempel
Bay	Baai	Baie	Bucht
Beach	Strand	Plage	Strand
Beacon	Baken	Balise	Bake
Bight	Bocht	Anse	Bay
Binoculars	Kijker	Jumelles	Fernglas
Board	Slag	Bordée	Schlage
Black	Zwart	Noir	Schwarz
Boatyard	Jachtwerf	Chantier	Yachtwerft
Breakwater	Golfbreker	Brise-lames	Wellenbrecher
Bridge	Brug	Pont	Brucke
(fixed)	(Vaste brug)	(Pont fixe)	(Feste brucke)
(lifting)	(Beweegbare brug)	(Pont basculant)	(Hubbrucke)
(swing)	(Draaibare brug)	(Pont tournant)	(Drehbrucke)
Buoy	Ton, boei	Bouée	Tonne, Boje
Cable (distance of approx 183m)	Kabellengte	Encablure	Kebellange
Causeway	Straatweg (door het water)	Chaussée	Damm
Castle	Kasteel, slot	Château	Schloss
Channel	Vaarwater	Chenal	Fahrwasser
Chart	Zeekaart	Carte marine	Seekarte
Chart Datum	Reductievlak: kaartpeil	Zero des cartes	Karennull
Church	Kerk	Eglise	Kirche
Cliff	Steile rots	Falaise	Felsen am Seeufer
Conspicuous	Opvallend	Visible, en evidence	Aufflallig
Course	Koers	Cap, route	Kurs
Coastguard	Kustwacht	Garde, Côtière	Kustenwache
Creek	Kreek	Crique	Kleine Bucht
Customs	Douane	Douane	Zoll
Depth	Diepte	Profondeur	Tiefe
Degree	Graad	Degre	Grad
Diesel oil	Dieselolie	Gas-oil, mazout	Diesel-Kraftstoff
Dolphin	Dukdarf, meerpaal	Duc d'Albe	Dalben, Dukdalben
Draught	Diepgang	Profondeur	Wassertiefe
Dredged	Gebaggerd vaarwater	Chenal dragué	Gebaggerte fahrrinne
Dries	Droogvalland	Assèche	Trockengallend
East	Oost	Est	Ost
Ebb	Eb	Marée descendante	Ebbe
Echo sounder	Echolood	Echo sondeur	Echolot
Eddy	Draaikolk	Tourbillon	Stromwirbel
Entrance	Ingang, zeegat	Entrée	Einfahrt
Estuary	Mond	Estuair	Flussmundung
Fair tide	Stroom mee	Courant favorable or portant	Mitlaufender Strom
Fairway	Vaargeul	Chenal	Telweg
Ferry	Veer	Bac, ferry	Fahre
Flagstaff	Vlaggestok	Mât	Flaggenmast

East Coast Rivers

ENGLISH	DUTCH	FRENCH	GERMAN
Flashing light	Schitterlicht	Feu a éclats	Blinkfeuer
Flood	Vloed	Marée montante	Flut
Ford	Waadbare plaats	Gué	Durchwaten
Foreshore	Droogvallend strand	Côte découvrant à marée basse	Küstenvorland
Foul tide	Tegenstroom	Courant contraire or debout	Gegenstrom
Fuel	Brandstof	Carburant	Kraftstoffe
Green	Groen	Vert	Grun
Groyne	Golfbreker	Brise-lames	Wellenbrecher
Gully	Goot	Goulet	Graben
Gunnery Range	Ballistiek	Artillerie	Artilleriewissenschaft
Gutway	Goot	Goulet	Graben
Handbearing compass	Handpeilkompas	Compas de relevement	Handpeilkompass
Harbourmaster	Havenmeester	Chef **or** Capitaine de port	Hafenkapitan
Hard	Hard	Débarquement	Landung
Headland	Voorgebergte	Promontoire	Vorgebirge
Height, headroom	Doorvaarthoogte	Tirant d'air	Durchfahrtshöhe
High Water	Hoogwater	Pleine mer	Hochwasser
Hill	Heuvel	Colline	Hügel
Horizontal stripes	Horizontal gestreept	à bandes horizontales	Waagerecht gestreift
Horse	Droogte	Basse	Untief
Island	Eiland	Ile	Insel
Jetty	Pier	Jetée	Anlegesteg
Knot	Knoop	Noeud	Knoten
Landing	Ontscheping	Débarquement	Landung
Launderette	Wasserette	Laverie	Waschsalon
Leading Line	Geleidelijn	Alignement	Leitlinie
Lead	Lood	Plomb de sonde	Lot
Lifeboat	Reddingboot	Bateau de sauvetage	Rettungboots
Lighthouse	Lichttoren, vuurtoren	Phare	Leuchtfurm
Light Vessel	Lichtschip	Bateau-phare	Feuerschiff
Lobster	Zeekreeft	Homard	Hummer
Lock	Sluis	Écluse, sas	Schleuse
Low Water	Laagwater	Basse mer	Niedrigwasser
Magnetic	Megnetisch	Magnetique	Mißweisend
Marks	Merkteken	Parcour	Bahnmarke
Marsh	Moeras	Marais	Sumpf
Metes	Geleidelijn	Alignement	Leitlinie
Middleground	Middelgronden	Bancs médians	Scheidingstonnen
Mooring	Meerboei	Bouée de corps-mort	Ankerboje
Mud	Modder	Vase/Boue	Schlick, Schlamm
Narrow	Nauw	Etroit	Eng(e)
Navigable	Bevaarbaar	Navigable	Befahrbare
Neaps	Doodtij	Morte eau	Nippitide
Occulting	Onderbroken	Occultations	Unterbrochenes
Offing	Open zee	Le large	Legerwall
Oil	Olie	Huile	Schimierol
Orange	Oranje	Orange	Orange
Oyster	Oester	Huître	Auster
Paraffin	Petroleum	Pétrole	Petroleum
Petrol	Benzine	Essence	Benzin
Perch	Steekbaken	Perches, pieu	Pricken
Piles	Palen remmingwerk	Poteaux	Pfahl
Pilot	Loods	Pilot	Lotsen
Pier	Pier	Jetee	Pier
Pontoon	Ponton	Ponton	Ponton
Port	Bakboord	Babord	Backbord
Post Office	Postkantoor	La Poste	Postamt
Quay	Kaai	Quai	Kai
Railway	Spoorweg	Chemin de fer	Eisenbahn
Radio Beacon	Radiobaken	Pylone de TSF	Funkmast
Range (of tide)	Verval	Amplitude	Tidenhub

ENGLISH	DUTCH	FRENCH	GERMAN
Red	Rood	Rouge	Rot
Repairs	Reparaties	Réparation	Ausbesserung
Riding Light	Ankerlicht	Feu de mouillage	Ankerlampe
Rocks	Rotsen	Rochers	Klippen, Felsen
Sailmaker	Zeilmaker	Voilier	Segelmacherei
Sand	Zand	Sable	Sand
Saltings	Zouttuin	Marais	Sumpf
Shelving	Hellen	Incline	Neigung
Shingle (shingly)	Grind,Keisteen	Galets	Grober Kies
Shops	Winkels	Magasins	Kaufladen
Shoal	Droogte	Haut fond	Untiefe
Showers	Douche	Douche	Dusche
Slipway	Sleephelling	Cale de halage	Slipp, Helling
South	Zuid	Sud	Süd
Spit	Landtong	Pointe de terre	Landzunge
Springs (tides)	Springtij	Vive eau, grande marée	Springtide
Staithe	Kade	Quai	Kai
Starboard	Stuurboord	Tribord	Steuerbord
Steep-to	Steil	Côte accore	Steil
Stores	Voorraad	Provisions	Vorrate
Swatchway	Doorgang	Couloir/passage	Passage
Take the ground	Aan de grond	Echoue	Auf grund sitzen
Tanker	Tanker, Tankschip	Bateau citerne	Tanker, Tankschiff
Topmark	Topteken	Voyant	Toppzeichen
Town	Stad	Ville	Stadt
Tortuous	Bochtig	Tortueux	Gewunden
Vertical stripes	Verticaal gestreept	à bandes verticales	Senkrecht gestreift
Village	Dorp	Village	Dorf
Visitor's berth	Aanlegplaats (Bezockers)	Visiteur	Festmacheplatz
Water	Water	l'eau	Wasser
Weather	Weer	du temps	Wetter
West	West	Ouest	West
Wharf	Aanlegplaats	Debarcadere	Werft
Withy	Buigzaam en sterk	Perches, pieux	Pricken
Wreck	Wrak	Épave	Wrack
Yacht Club	Jacht Club, Zeilvereniging	Yacht Club, Club Nautique	Yacht Klub
Yellow	Geel	Jaune	Gelb

Bibliography

Several references have been made to books relating to the rivers and creeks of the Thames Estuary and this is a list of some of those and other books that are worth seeking through a public library if they are out of print.

Arnott, WG   **Suffolk Estuary**, published by Norman Adlard (1950)
                      Alde Estuary, Norman Adlard (1952)
                      Orwell Estuary, Norman Adlard (1954)

Benham, Hervey   **Last Stronghold of Sail**, George Harrap (1947)

Copping, AE   **Gotty and the Guv'nor**, first published by T Nelson & Sons and then by Terence Dalton (1987)

Cowper, Frank   **Sailing Tours Part 1**, first published 1882 and then by Ashford Press in 1985

Durham, Dick   **The Last Sailorman**, Terence Dalton (1989)

Emmett A and M   **Blackwater Men**, Seax Books (1982)

Frost, Michael   **Boadicea CK213**, Angus & Robertson (1974)

Griffiths, Maurice   **The Magic of the Swatchways**, first published by Edward Arnold (1932) and Adlard Coles (1986)
                      Ten Small Yachts, Edward Arnold (1933)
                      Swatchways and Little Ships, George Allen & Unwin (1971) and Adlard Coles (1986)

Innes, Hammond   **East Anglia**, Hodder & Stoughton (1986)

Leather, John   **The Salty Shore**, Terence Dalton (1979)
                      The Sailor's Coast, Barrie & Jenkins (1979)

Lewis, John   **A Taste for Sailing**, Terence Dalton (1989)

Roberts, Bob   **Coasting Bargemaster**, Edward Arnold (1949) and Terence Dalton (1985)
                      A Slice of Suffolk, Terence Dalton (1978)

Ransome, Arthur   **Secret Water**, Jonathan Cape (1939) and then by Penguin Books

Tripp, Alker   **Suffolk Sea Borders**, Bodley Head (1926) and Maritime Press (1972)
                      Shoalwater and Fairway, Bodley Head (1924) and Maritime Press (1972)

White, Archie   **The Tideways and Byways of Essex and Suffolk**, Edward Arnold (1948)

A *Yachting Monthly* Pilot. East Coast Rivers is published by IPC Magazines Ltd of King's Reach Tower, Stamford Street, London SE1 9LS, and printed in Hong Kong by World Print. Conditions of sale: this publication shall not, without the written consent of the publishers first being given, be lent, resold, hired out, or otherwise disposed of by way of trade at more than the recommended selling price shown on the back cover and that it shall not be lent, resold, or hired out or otherwise disposed of in a mutilated condition or in any unauthorised cover by way of trade or annexed to or as part of any publication or advertising literary, or pictorial matter whatsoever.